This is the season of the restoration of all things. Let it begin in your life with Joshua Mills's heavenly revelation in his new book, *7 Divine Mysteries: Supernatural Secrets to Unlimited Abundance.*

—*Sid Roth*
Host, *It's Supernatural!*

Jesus said, *"I have come that they may have life, and that they may have it more abundantly"* (John 10:10), but many believers struggle to survive on a daily basis. The secret to an abundant life continues to remain a mystery to them. That is why I am so excited about the release of this new book by my good friend Joshua Mills, *7 Divine Mysteries: Supernatural Secrets to Unlimited Abundance.* Joshua lays out a clear, concise path for living a supernatural life with God's divine and supernatural provision. You will discover the spiritual keys to abundance and victory— no matter what your circumstances happen to be at the moment.

—*Joan Hunter*
Author and evangelist

Jesus invites us *all* into the fullness of His abundant life—a message we need to hear more and more as the end-times intensify and life in the natural world becomes increasingly unstable. A life of miraculous abundance is not reserved only for certain people or for the "good times" in life. It is for *every* believer, with *any* background, in *any* situation. In *7 Divine Mysteries: Supernatural Secrets to Unlimited Abundance,* Joshua Mills opens up the realm of supernatural provision for spirit, soul, and body so you can enter into the riches of heaven, being blessed and becoming a channel of blessing to others for the kingdom of God. Don't ever doubt that God loves you and has a plan to bless and proper you—to the glory of His name!

—*Katie Souza*
Author, teacher, and healing evangelist
Host, *Healing Your Soul: Real Keys to the Miraculous* television program

Our God is the Lord of the breakthrough! He is ready to lead you into overflowing abundance if you will enter the place of supernatural provision He has prepared for you. In his new book, Joshua Mills guides you into the revelation of 7 *Divine Mysteries* to unlimited abundance for every area of your life, with chapters like "Divine Mystery #1: Heavenly Vision Is a Pathway for Provision" and "Divine Mystery #5: Generous Believing Produces Generous Receiving." This is not a time to be complacent in your walk with God. This is not a time to be discouraged about what your circumstances look like or the troubles you see around you. This is the time to rise up, overcome, and be blessed to be a blessing!

—*Tom and Jane Hamon*
Senior Leaders, Vision Church @ Christian International

The abundant life truly holds mysteries within it. I have become aware of many of these mysteries firsthand as I have journeyed with the Lord in more than forty-five years of living for Him. Joshua Mills's book 7 *Divine Mysteries* will connect you to the heart of God and also His unending and amazing provision—no matter what happens within the world's economy. This book has been written for such a time as this!

—*Patricia King*
Author, minister, media host, and producer

I am so excited for you! 7 *Divine Mysteries* is more than just a good book or a great read. It is a glorious God-invitation to step into the abundant life Jesus has provided for you—*a life of unlimited abundance!* God loves to share His secrets with His friends (see John 15:15). These friends of God are often the ones He chooses to not only share His divine mysteries with but also manifest the miracles of His mysteries in their lives in a way that creates a holy hunger for more of Him! When the apostle Paul spoke of those who would steward and distribute the divine mysteries of God throughout the earth, he pointed to a life of surrender and the fruit of faithfulness as necessary prerequisites (see 1 Corinthians 4:1–2). Joshua Mills is a friend of God, and in that place of friendship, faithfulness, and sacrificial surrender, God has imparted to him and his family beautiful truths and supernatural secrets to help you access the life of abundance that God has prepared for you.

—*Jason Hooper*
Senior Pastor, King's Way Church
www.kingswayal.com

When I hear the Scripture *"For the kingdom of God is not a matter of talk but of power"* (1 Corinthians 4:20), I think of Joshua Mills. Joshua is the real deal, full of faith, with signs and wonders accompanying. Joshua lives a supernatural life with, and in, Jesus. When he speaks, there's a spirit of expectancy in the atmosphere, as if anything can happen—and Jesus doesn't disappoint. After reading *7 Divine Mysteries*, you will walk in greater realms of the glory of Jesus!

—*Quincy Good Star*
Quincy Good Star Ministries
www.quincygoodstar.com

For many people, *7 Divine Mysteries* is going to be their breakthrough. I believe that the wisdom, experience, testimony, revelation, and anointing in this book are going to redirect your mind, heart, and life toward abundance. This is the kingdom. This is the grace of God. This is the blessing of the heirs of God. I eagerly and joyfully recommend that you carve out the time to take on Joshua Mills's powerful new book. This is your life-changing moment!

—*Ryan Rufus*
The Grace Bible Commentary video series
www.NewNatureMinistries.org

In his new book, *7 Divine Mysteries: Supernatural Secrets to Unlimited Abundance*, Joshua Mills has pulled back the veil to uncover the secrets of living in plenitude. As a skilled musician uses musical notes to compose a masterpiece, Joshua uses written words to orchestrate God's glorious revelation of abundance. Filled with keen insight, powerful principles, and life-changing testimonies, this book will catapult you into another dimension of God's blessings.

—*Andrew Towe*
Lead Pastor, Ramp Church Chattanooga
Author, *The Triple Threat Anointing*

I have known my friend Joshua Mills for many years. He is a man of integrity and character, a loving father, and a faithful husband. Joshua has a gift of insight that pulls keys from God's realm and presents them in such a way that any reader can step into the truths of his message. In *7 Divine Mysteries*, Joshua teaches us how to shift into a greater, more empowered, abundant life so that we don't just "exist" on this earth but rather tap into a higher realm of supernatural living. This is a walk that will cause us to realize the full potential of God's intent for our destiny, purpose, and design. You were made for more, and as you read and put into practice these kingdom principles, I am convinced that your life will flourish in Jesus and touch the world around you.

—*Andrew Billings*
Senior Pastor, Dwelling Place OC
Huntington Beach, Orange County, CA

There is simply no one we know who is better qualified to write a book entitled *7 Divine Mysteries: Supernatural Secrets to Unlimited Abundance* than Joshua Mills. It is an honor and joy to wholeheartedly recommend this book to you. We have personally known and ministered with Joshua and Janet Mills for over a decade, and we have greatly gleaned from their lives and ministry. We have seen firsthand the truths and revelations in this book played out in their lives. *7 Divine Mysteries* contains anointed and powerful revelation coupled with Joshua's childlike awe and easy-to-read communication style, which makes it a dynamic catalyst for life-changing breakthrough in your own life. Get ready to never be the same.

—*Ben and Jodie Hughes*
Pour It Out Ministries
www.pouritout.org
Authors, *When God Breaks In* and *The King's Decree*

Joshua Mills's diligence in seeking out a matter is once again impacting the body of Christ in a significant way through his new book on unlimited abundance, *7 Divine Mysteries*. Joshua is the real deal. Over the past seven years, I have relationally observed the continual increase of abundance and true wealth in his life. I have been impacted not only by his masterful teaching, but also by the evidence of fruit. Be prepared for impartation as you dive into his teaching on abundance. Our reliance on God is where the secrets are found to bring about positive change. Joshua's book is a must-read for all who want to impact this world for the kingdom of God!

—*Robert Kinsella*
Advisor, entrepreneur, and minister
CEO and Founder, KBV International

Joshua Mills does it again! *7 Divine Mysteries* is another must-have book that builds your faith, challenges your everyday thinking to go higher and deeper with God, and motivates you to press into the supernatural realm that is available to all of us. We love having Joshua minister at our church because not only is there a strong impartation of the supernatural power of God, but the body is encouraged to press into the Holy Spirit and experience the glory of God daily!

—*Mel and Desiree Ayres*
Pastors and Founders, In His Presence Church, Los Angeles
Producers of multiple music projects, including *Witness*
Author (Desiree Ayers), *Beyond the Flame* and *God Hunger*

In *7 Divine Mysteries: Supernatural Secrets to Unlimited Abundance*, Joshua Mills provides readers with thorough yet practical keys to unlock God's promises in their own lives. I have witnessed firsthand how Joshua and his wife, Janet, have personally used these keys to successfully move in God's abundance. I genuinely admire their faith and consider them both role models and forerunners in this area. Joshua's latest book provides invaluable insights that, once applied, will shift the body of Christ from surviving to thriving. It is time for believers to receive all that their Father wishes to give them. Following these supernatural secrets will unlock His unlimited abundance!

—*Joanna Adams*
Author and Senior Pastor, *Eagles' Nest Fellowship*
Eagle Worldwide Ministries, Ontario, Canada

As ministers, when we need to have our faith stirred, check the elasticity of our wineskins, or be reminded of the wonders of our wondrous God, we look toward Brother Joshua Mills. The sheer faith that is unlocked while reading the testimonies Joshua shares is enough to set you ablaze! For far too long, the church has suffocated the abundant realm of God that we clearly see in the Bible! Page after page of the Bible testifies of God's abundant provision for His children, both in the Spirit and in the natural! Joshua has a breaker anointing to impart the gift of faith to the body of Christ. *7 Divine Mysteries: Supernatural Secrets to Unlimited Abundance* is your personal invitation to tap the untapped wells of wealth breakthrough! This book is a door-busting, poverty-breaking, abundance-manifesting POWER tool in the hands of a hungry believer! Get ready for your "next" because, friend, you're holding it in your hands.

—*Zac and Natalie Breckenridge*
Founding Pastors, LifeBridge Jonesboro
Jonesboro, AR

When Jesus spoke to Peter, *"And I will give you the keys of the kingdom of heaven…,"* He also equipped Peter with the instruction manual for those keys, saying, *"…and whatever you bind on earth will be bound in heaven, and whatever you loose on earth will be loosed in heaven"* (Matthew 16:19 NKJV). Keys of the kingdom are being discovered today! Joshua Mills gives us seven powerful keys in his newest book, *7 Divine Mysteries: Supernatural Secrets to Unlimited Abundance.* I highly encourage you to glean from Joshua the supernatural keys heaven is releasing right now!

—*Jamie Galloway*
Jamie Galloway Ministries
Author, *Secrets of the Seer*

7
DIVINE MYSTERIES

Whitaker House Books and Resources by Joshua Mills

7 Divine Mysteries: Supernatural Secrets to Unlimited Abundance
7 Divine Mysteries audiobook
7 Divine Mysteries Study Guide

Creative Glory: Embracing the Realm of Divine Expression
Creative Glory audiobook
Creative Glory Study Guide

Moving in Glory Realms: Exploring Dimensions of Divine Presence
Moving in Glory Realms audiobook
Moving in Glory Realms Study Guide

Power Portals: Awaken Your Connection to the Spirit Realm
Power Portals audiobook
Power Portals Study Guide

Seeing Angels: How to Recognize and Interact with Your
Heavenly Messengers
Seeing Angels audiobook
Seeing Angels Study Guide

Additional Audios

Activating Angels in Your Life
Experience His Glory
Opening the Portals
Receive Your Healing

Devotional Resources

Activating Angels 365 (perpetual desktop calendar)
The Glory: Scriptures and Prayers to Manifest God's Presence in Your Life
The Power of His Names (77 devotional cards and guidebook)

7
DIVINE
MYSTERIES

SUPERNATURAL SECRETS TO
UNLIMITED ABUNDANCE

JOSHUA MILLS

WHITAKER
HOUSE

Unless otherwise indicated, all Scripture quotations are taken from the *King James Version Easy Read Bible*, KJVER®, © 2001, 2007, 2010, 2015 by Whitaker House. Used by permission. All rights reserved. Scripture quotations marked (KJV) are taken from the King James Version of the Holy Bible. Scripture quotations marked (NIV) are taken from the *Holy Bible, New International Version*®, NIV®, © 1973, 1978, 1984, 2011 by Biblica, Inc.® Used by permission of Zondervan. All rights reserved worldwide. www.zondervan.com. The "NIV" and "New International Version" are trademarks registered in the United States Patent and Trademark Office by Biblica, Inc. Scripture quotations marked (AMP) are taken from *The Amplified® Bible*, © 2015 by The Lockman Foundation, La Habra, CA. Used by permission. (www.Lockman.org). All rights reserved. Scripture quotations marked (AMPC) are taken from *The Amplified® Bible, Classic Edition*, © 1954, 1958, 1962, 1964, 1965, 1987 by The Lockman Foundation. Used by permission (www.Lockman.org). All rights reserved. Scripture quotations marked (NKJV) are taken from the *New King James Version*, © 1979, 1980, 1982 by Thomas Nelson, Inc. Used by permission. All rights reserved. Scripture quotations marked (NLT) are taken from the *Holy Bible, New Living Translation*, copyright © 1996, 2004, 2015 by Tyndale House Foundation. Used by permission of Tyndale House Publishers, Inc., Carol Stream, Illinois 60188. All rights reserved. Scripture quotations marked (TPT) are taken from The *Passion Translation*,® © 2017, 2018, 2020 by Passion & Fire Ministries, Inc. Used by permission. All rights reserved. (thePassionTranslation.com).

The forms LORD and GOD (in small caps) in Bible quotations represent the Hebrew name for God *Yahweh* (Jehovah), while *Lord* and *God* normally represent the name *Adonai*, in accordance with the Bible version used.

Boldface type in the Scripture quotations indicates the author's emphasis.

7 DIVINE MYSTERIES:
Supernatural Secrets to Unlimited Abundance

International Glory Ministries
JoshuaMills.com
info@joshuamills.com

ISBN: 978-1-64123-650-8 • eBook ISBN: 978-1-64123-651-5

Printed in the United States of America
© 2021 by Joshua Mills

Whitaker House • 1030 Hunt Valley Circle • New Kensington, PA 15068
www.whitakerhouse.com

Library of Congress Control Number: 2021933241

1 2 3 4 5 6 7 8 9 10 11 ᴜ 28 27 26 25 24 23 22 21

DEDICATION

In memory of my spiritual father, the late Pastor William C. Wilson, and dedicated to my spiritual mother, Beverly C. Wilson, who both taught me about God's abundance and demonstrated it through their lavish generosity and spiritual impartation toward me.

I would like to also dedicate this book to the spiritually hungry ones—those of you who are not satisfied with the status quo. You are the forerunners, ever pressing forward, running the race set before you, knowing there is always more in God. For you, this book has been written, and because of you, I'm eternally grateful. Let's dive into all of the mysteries of God and make them known on earth!

These are the things God has revealed to us by his Spirit. The Spirit searches all things, even the deep things of God.

(1 Corinthians 2:10 NIV)

ACKNOWLEDGMENTS

Each of the books I have written has flowed from supernatural encounters that were first written in my heart. This book is no different. The teachings and testimonies I present are the result of more than twenty years of walking in these divine mysteries and watching them unfold in a revelatory way with God's unlimited abundance.

Of course, many times, the way God brings us into new things is through the impartation of the words, prayers, and ministries of spiritual pioneers who have gone before us to lead the way. I must acknowledge the anointed ministries that helped to open my heart and understanding to this divine realm of abundance in the early years of my ministry. Dr. Rodney and Adonica Howard-Browne: I am forever indebted to you for your commitment to God's Word of prosperity and the Spirit of revival. Rev. John Shiver: Thank you for your teaching on giving and what it will do in the life of a believer. You are one of the reasons I became addicted to a lifestyle of generosity. Dr. Jane Lowder: Thank you for believing in what God was birthing in me in the very early years—and for prophesying about so much of my future. You helped cast vision in my spirit, which has manifested in the outward provisions of my life. Patricia King: Your constant friendship, counsel, encouragement, and godly teaching have helped to build a framework of supernatural abundance for Janet and me. You have not only spoken truth into our lives, but your life has been an example to us, and you have set an exemplary path for us to follow. I must also acknowledge the teachings of Rev. D. Karl and Cheryl Thomas, Kenneth E. Hagin, Charles Capps, Charles and Frances Hunter, Bishop Clint Brown, Kenneth and Gloria Copeland, Dr. Oral Roberts, and Ruth Ward Heflin. These ministries laid an excellent foundation of deep spiritual truths upon which my life and ministry have been built. I want to thank each one of you, and for those who are already in heaven, you know and recognize the legacy that continues. Your impact and influence have marked me in a profound way.

I also want to thank each and every one of our Miracle Worker partners who faithfully commit to praying and financially sowing into the work of this ministry on a monthly basis. Your prayers are deeply felt, and your continued support has enabled me to put the Spirit's revelations onto the printed page. My prayer is that you would be immensely blessed and that your life would be made one thousand times more abundant! This book is for you. Study each page, master each mystery, and walk in every abundance.

Finally, I want to thank all the people who have made this book possible, especially my team at Whitaker House—Bob Whitaker Jr., Christine Whitaker, Jim Armstrong, and Becky Speer. And, of course, thank you to my wonderful editors Lois Puglisi, Angela R. Shears, and Harold McDougal for your skillful work in grooming and properly fine-tuning the message of this book. All of your anointed efforts are producing eternal fruit as people capture, embrace, and fully walk in the divine mysteries. I can hardly wait to hear the testimonies of those who begin manifesting unlimited abundance because of your Spirit-led labors!

CONTENTS

FOREWORD

In my book *A Divine Revelation of Heaven*, I describe how Jesus took me in the Spirit to heaven and, for ten consecutive nights, revealed to me many of its magnificent glories. In one of those visits, an angel showed me God's heavenly storehouses. When I inquired about one of these storehouses, the angel told me that its rooms were filled with blessings that are available for God's people.

Then, Jesus told me, "The blessings contained here await the belief of those on earth. All they have to do is believe and receive—believe that I am the Lord Jesus Christ and that I am able to do these things, and receive My gifts."

This message about God's storehouses of abundant blessings is just as important for believers today as when I first wrote that book. Too many of God's people don't realize the treasures that our heavenly Father longs to provide for us, if we will only receive them. Because of this, they have not entered into the abundant life that Jesus promises us. Here is how I described God's desire for us to enter into His life of abundance:

Heaven is perfect purity, and God wants to purify His saints on earth so they will enjoy heaven's atmosphere. Heaven is fullness of joy, and God desires to give joy to His people on earth. Heaven is everlasting freedom, and God longs for His people to have deliverance while on earth. Heaven is perfect wholeness, and God wants to heal His people here on earth. Heaven is complete security, and God wants His people to feel confident and secure here on earth. Heaven is fruition and fulfillment, and God desires that His people be fulfilled on earth.

When Jesus instructed us to pray that God's *"will be done on earth as it is in heaven"* (Matthew 6:10), He revealed that God wants us to have a taste of heaven here on earth!

Saints, the Lord has storehouses of blessings just for you. They are waiting in heaven for you to claim them and to receive them now, here on earth. God wants to save you. He wants to deliver you. He wants to heal you. He wants you to know *"the peace of God, which surpasses all understanding"* (Philippians 4:7). He wants you to experience a lasting *"joy inexpressible and full of glory"* (1 Peter 1:8).[1]

God desires for His mysteries of abundance to become divine revelations for every believer so they can enter into His wonderful, eternal provisions!

In *7 Divine Mysteries: Supernatural Secrets to Unlimited Abundance*, my friend Joshua Mills beautifully illuminates these heavenly blessings and explains how we can receive them today. We must understand that heaven's storehouses can be accessed by God's people who ask in faith and in the name of Jesus.

I met Joshua Mills for the first time a little over a decade ago. We knew about each other's ministries but had never had an opportunity to meet, so I was delighted when he called and asked if we could have lunch together. We had a precious time of sharing our heart for souls and the work of the Lord. At that lunch, I laid hands upon Joshua and prayed for him, and a great anointing flowed. Joshua felt

1. Mary K. Baxter, *A Divine Revelation of Heaven* (New Kensington, PA: Whitaker House, 1998), pp. 54–56.

an impartation being released into his life for an increase of divine revelation and heavenly encounters.

Soon after this, I was invited to tape some programs for a Christian television show in Los Angeles. Joshua also came to the studio because he would be taping programs there as well. We were each unaware that the other would be at the studio that day, but God had arranged this second meeting for His divine purposes. I asked Joshua to join me on the last program I taped. We spoke about angels and the abundance of God's glory realm. Later, many testimonies came in as a result of those programs from people who were set free to experience God in a greater and deeper way.

Over the years, I have enjoyed a wonderful friendship with Joshua. I have read all of his books, and his teachings have helped me to understand even more about my own supernatural experiences. I know that God will bless you mightily in all areas of your life as you reach out in faith to access the overflowing abundance of heaven's storehouses!

—*Mary K. Baxter*

PREFACE:
EVERYONE LOVES A GOOD MYSTERY!

W hen I was a young child, it seemed to me that the world held so much mystery. (I still feel that way!) I spent my days reading *Ripley's Believe It or Not!* comics, raising otherworldly Sea-Monkeys as bedroom pets, and playing with intriguing Mexican jumping beans that bounced around for weeks until their shells "miraculously" developed holes in them, and they no longer jumped. Ha! There was so much mystery and wonder to it all.

As I grew a bit older, Thursday became my favorite day of the week because my brother, Matthew, and I would watch the television show *Matlock*. After all, who doesn't love a good, clean, whodunit crime show?

Everybody loves a good mystery! Mystery is everywhere in our natural world, reflecting the mystery of our Creator and of the spiritual realm. I was fascinated the first time I visited Florida and saw a sand dollar on the beach. At a local souvenir shop, I even found a postcard with a poem explaining how this special shell portrayed the sacred message of Jesus Christ's birth, death, and resurrection. Here is one version of this poem, whose author is unknown:

"The Legend of the Sand Dollar"

There's a lovely little legend
That I would like to tell
Of the birth and death of Jesus,
Found in this lowly shell.

If you examine closely,
You'll see that you find here
Four nail holes and a fifth one,
Made by a Roman's spear.

On one side the Easter lily,
Its center is the star
That appeared unto the shepherds
And led them from afar.

The Christmas Poinsettia
Etched on the other side
Reminds us of His birthday,
Our joyous Christmastide.

Now break the center open,
And here you will release
The five white doves awaiting
To spread good will and peace.

This simple little symbol
Christ left for you and me
To help to spread His gospel
Through all eternity.

Yes, everywhere in nature, we see the fingerprints of God in His wondrous works, leaving us clues about Himself and His ways. And as we search the Bible, God's Word, we discover divine mysteries throughout the Scriptures as well. The spirit realm is a mysterious domain.

When Jesus was on earth, He spoke in parables so that only those who were discerning enough could decode the messages about God's supernatural kingdom that He was delivering. In many ways, Jesus's use of this story form guarded the revelations and prevented their misuse by those who wanted nothing more than to destroy the ministry of Christ and His followers. (See, for example, Matthew 13:10–15.)

I wrote *7 Divine Mysteries: Supernatural Secrets to Unlimited Abundance* because God wants to share His eternal secrets with His people, but many believers have not searched for them or fully understood them. Jesus told His disciples, *"You are permitted to understand the secrets of the Kingdom of Heaven…"* (Matthew 13:11 NLT). And we read in Proverbs, *"It is the glory of God to conceal a matter; to search out a matter is the glory of kings"* (25:2 NIV). We have been made *"kings and priests to God"* (Revelation 1:6), and it is our privilege to discover all the hidden mysteries of the glory realm. This book is about God's powerful revelation of a number of these mysteries in His Word—*supernatural secrets to unlimited abundance*. I'm excited to share with you what I have learned from the Spirit regarding these secrets.

In this day, God is making known to us how to tap into unlimited abundance so that we can walk in the wealth of heaven every single day of our lives. Again, these are *mysteries* because supernatural secrets are hidden from the natural mind and only available to those who are willing to operate by the mind of the Spirit. Once these mysteries are unlocked for your heart and mind through this book, I believe that you will begin to see them unlocked in your life as you follow the leading of God's Spirit.

I have titled this book *7 Divine Mysteries* because, in addition to the foundational principles of abundance that we will survey in chapter 1, I have identified seven supernatural mysteries in God's Word for manifesting unlimited heavenly riches. The number seven is significant in the spirit realm, and this significance is reflected in our physical world. For example, traditionally, in nature, there are seven oceans, seven continents, and seven colors of the rainbow. In the Bible, the number seven is God's perfect number. The menorah in the tabernacle and temple had seven candles (see Exodus 25:21–39), and in the book of Revelation, we read about seven angels over the seven churches, seven stars, seven trumpets, and seven seals (see, for example, Revelation 1:20; 5:1; 8:2, 6).

We also see the sevenfold Spirit of God described with the following seven attributes: the Spirit of the Lord, the Spirit of wisdom, the Spirit of understanding, the Spirit of counsel, the Spirit of might, the Spirit of knowledge, and the Spirit of the fear of the Lord. (See for example, Revelation 1:4; Isaiah 11:2.)

The number seven represents divine completion, as in the seven days of creation. I also believe it symbolizes God's design for unity between earth and heaven—the *"four corners of the earth"* (Isaiah 11:12; Revelation 7:1) joining with the three-in-One Godhead—the natural realm perfectly connecting with the divine supernatural realm through the redemptive work of Christ.

Additionally, the number seven is the number of rest, as in the Sabbath rest of the seventh day. As we come to understand the seven divine mysteries of supernatural abundance, we must learn how to rest in God because there is an ease in the glory. I firmly believe that the key to the success of our ministry and our ability to do what God has called us to do has been the revelation of His glory and the abundance that can be discovered in this realm.

The seven divine mysteries will unfold to you through each successive chapter in this book:

Heavenly Vision Is a Pathway for Provision
What You Say Creates a Way
The Word You Work Will Work for You
What You Sow, You Will Grow
Generous Believing Produces Generous Receiving
Angel Power Makes Abundance Shower
Generational Investing Brings Generational Blessing

God has revealed to me that the manifestation of divine abundance depends on my reliance on Him and Him alone. I desire that you, too, would learn how to rest in this revelation. A life of abundance is solely dependent upon living for Him and participating in agreement with His everlasting Word, the Bible—our life-giving source of truth and wisdom from the eternal God.

CHAPTER 1

YOU CAN MANIFEST ABUNDANCE

"Then God blessed them and said, 'Be fruitful and multiply....'"
—Genesis 1:28 (NLT)

SUPERNATURAL MYSTERIES 101

Imagine that you are a detective who is seeking to solve a mystery. To do so, you need a unique mindset that can see both the big picture and the fine details that unlock the secrets to the puzzle. You also need compelling evidence on which to base your conclusions.

It is the same way for us when we seek to uncover the supernatural mysteries that God has given in His Word and revealed through His Spirit. And one vital area of God's supernatural mysteries concerns how to live in *unlimited abundance*.

As "spiritual detectives," we first need to step back and see the whole scene: What is the environment of divine provision? What are the foundational truths that apply to all supernatural mysteries of abundance? The answers will set us on the right path to discovery.

Second, we need to hone in on the fine details of some specific divine mysteries. What further clues will unlock their secrets? These fine details will emerge as we dig deeper to discover additional scriptural truths and principles about divine abundance.

Finally, we need to identify clear evidence of the laws of God's abundance in action. Our confirmation will come in the biblical record and in testimonies of the outworking of God's supernatural provision in people's lives today.

Together, all of these perspectives will enable us to enter into the tremendous wealth God has provided to bless us, people around us, and the world.

In this book, I share revelations concerning seven divine mysteries of unlimited abundance so that you can begin manifesting abundance in your life. These revelations, based on God's Word, will be life-shifting for you—if you listen, believe, and walk in the divine instructions they provide.

In chapter 1, we begin by exploring the biblical "big picture." We will discover spiritual principles of abundance that are the setting for all seven divine mysteries so that, when you reach the end of this book, you will have gained a comprehensive understanding of what it means to live an abundant life in Christ and know how to put these principles into practice. Without these foundational principles, you won't be able to move on to the fine details of unlocking each individual mystery. But when you establish these truths in your life, you will be able to live in the reality of divine abundance.

THE BIBLICAL "BIG PICTURE" OF ABUNDANCE

ABUNDANCE COMES FROM HEAVEN

To begin to understand the unlimited abundance God wants to give us, let's look at a familiar story from the Bible with new eyes—the eyes of a spiritual detective—and then see how God is still working His boundless abundance in a parallel way today.

Once, a great crowd followed Jesus into a sparsely populated place to hear more of His teachings, and when it came time to eat, there was nowhere for them to obtain food. The people's hunger moved the heart of Jesus. The disciples reported that a little boy had a few loaves of bread and two pieces of fish. (See John 6:8–9.)

> [Jesus] *said, "Bring them here to Me." Then He commanded the multitudes to sit down on the grass. And He took the five loaves and the two fish, and* **looking up to heaven***, He blessed and broke and gave the loaves to the disciples; and the disciples gave to the multitudes. So they all ate and were filled, and they took up twelve baskets full of the fragments that remained. Now those who had eaten were about five thousand men, besides women and children.*
>
> (Matthew 14:18–21 NKJV)

Jesus looked to heaven, not to earth, for supernatural provision. He wasn't looking in the natural; He was looking in the Spirit. And that's a key for us too. If all you see is lack, if there is poverty on every side, then it's time to look to heaven. Focus your eyes on the Author and the Finisher of your faith. (See Hebrews 12:2.) Doing so will begin to train you to see the big spiritual picture when it comes to receiving abundance.

After Jesus had looked to heaven, He blessed those few pieces of food, broke them, and gave them to His disciples. It was then up to the disciples to distribute the food, giving a portion to each person in that great multitude. Amazingly, everyone ate and was filled, and still they gathered up twelve full baskets of leftovers. I believe those twelve baskets represent every month of the year for us. In God's Word, we are promised His divine blessing in every season of life:

> *They are like trees planted along the riverbank,* **bearing fruit each season***. Their leaves never wither, and they prosper in all they do.*
>
> (Psalm 1:3 NLT)

No one had a way to make an official count that day, but those who had eaten were about five thousand men, not including the women and children who had accompanied them to hear Jesus teach.

Jesus had started with five small loaves of bread and two fish. It has been estimated that, to feed that many people and have food left over, it would have required about twenty thousand small loaves of bread common in that day and thousands of fish. What a great, creative, supernatural miracle of abundance from heaven! And it began with Jesus's loving concern for the needs of the people.

OVERFLOWING SPAGHETTI

The same type of heavenly abundance is available to us today when we look to heaven for our provision. Once, my wife, Janet, and I were with a ministry team in the Canadian Arctic in a northern village called Purvirnituq (POV for short), an Inuit community. We stayed in a hotel called the Novalinga, which was about the size of a small house. Each bedroom had the square footage of a medium-sized closet, so that when we opened the door to enter our room, we practically stumbled onto the single bed. Although the room was small, it had a little shelf where we could put some of our belongings, and we were thankful for the accommodations.

Along with Janet and me, a second ministry couple and another preacher were staying there. One day, after the morning meeting, we went back to the hotel, and Janet and the other pastor's wife decided to make some spaghetti for lunch.

The Inuits are very generous people, and we love them and their culture. What is theirs is yours, without question. In their northern communities, there is no need to knock on someone's door. You can just go right in, sit down at their table, fellowship with them, and eat their food.

As we were finishing our lunch preparations, in walked ten or twelve of the Inuit leaders, who were ready for lunch. What should we do? We had prepared only enough for ourselves, but we could not deny the others. We quickly decided to pray a prayer of multiplication over that food. We could think of no other option. There was no nearby store to run to and buy more food, and tradition demanded that everybody be fed.

We didn't need to feed five thousand men, plus women and children, as Jesus did, but we did need to feed about another dozen people! I actually like it when God puts us in these situations where we cannot turn to the natural but have to depend upon the supernatural. It is in such moments when we see miracles happen. If we try to work out a situation with our own ability, we miss the manifestation of God's ability. We miss His miraculous provision simply because we rely on ourselves.

Nowhere in the Bible does it say, "Trust in your own ability." In fact, it says just the opposite. We are not to trust in our own understanding. In everything, we are to lean on God, putting our faith in His matchless proficiency, trusting Him for His unlimited abundance. (See Proverbs 3:5–6.) God is more than able to do whatever it is that we need Him to do. He is more than enough—and He didn't disappoint us that day.

After we had prayed, we started dishing out the spaghetti. Everybody had enough, and we were all completely satisfied. The Inuit pastors were delighted that we had prepared such a wonderful banquet for them. To God be all the glory!

OUR GOD IS THE GOD OF ABUNDANCE

One of the truths I want you to deeply capture in your spirit is that our God is the God of abundance. The idea of living an overflowing life filled with every good and wonderful provision isn't the stuff of legends or fairytales. This idea comes directly from God Himself. He is the God of abundance, and the Scriptures prove it! Take, for example. these wonderful truths:

- The earth and everything in it belong to God. (See Psalm 24:1.)
- All the silver and gold belong to Him. (See Haggai 2:8.)
- God is the Rancher of all ranchers; all the animals are His. (See Psalm 50:10.)
- God's greatness is unlimited. (See Psalm 145:3.)
- *"Every good and every perfect gift"* comes from Him. (See James 1:17.)
- God oversees an innumerable host of angels. (See Revelation 5:11.)

And the list could go on.

When we think about abundance, the very first thing that should come to our minds is God. Everything about God is grand, overflowing, plentiful, and filled with abundance. In the Word, we're reminded, *"And God will generously provide all you need. Then you will always have everything you need and plenty left over to share with others"* (2 Corinthians 9:8–9 nlt). God is our true source of abundance!

ABUNDANCE FOR EVERY NEED

When we understand where our provision comes from, we can receive supernatural abundance in all areas of our lives—spiritual, physical, emotional, and intellectual—whenever we are in need and whenever we require resources to do all that God has called us to do.

When Janet and I were newlyweds, we lived in San Diego, California. At one point, our funds were quite low. We had only fifteen dollars in our bank account, and we were scraping together our coins to buy little things we needed. One day, we went to a meeting at our church and were impressed by God to contribute to the offering. At the close of the meeting, my good friend Paul Burke wanted a soda, and he asked me if I had enough change to lend him. I didn't really think I did, but acting out of instinct, I reached into my pocket and was very surprised to feel some paper money there. I definitely knew it hadn't been there before. "Wow!" I thought to myself, "I have a dollar."

When I pulled out the money to hand it to Paul, I was amazed to see that it was a one hundred dollar bill. God had supplied that money for me. No one else had put it there. I certainly would have felt the hand of anyone reaching so deeply into my pocket! This was God's creative glory at work to bring forth abundance in our finances. We thanked God and rejoiced in this heaven-sent money miracle.

I'm not saying that God is a counterfeiter; He doesn't counterfeit anything. But He knows where all money is to be found. It might be hidden under some floorboards. It might be laid up in a long-neglected attic. It might be buried somewhere under the sea. It might come from another very unexpected source. In fact, the Bible says that the wealth of the wicked is laid up for the righteous—meaning those who are in Christ. (See Proverbs 13:22.) Those who are focused on the things of God and are worshipping Him wholeheartedly have blessings coming from the heavenly realm. Our God of abundance knows how to send it to us.

God is an ever-increasing God. His glory is expanding every day, and He wants you to experience unlimited abundance in your life right now, here on earth. Contrary to popular belief, true abundance is not just about wealth accumulation. It is actually more about *flow*— God's provision flowing *to* you so that it can flow *through* you. It is about having plenty to meet your own spiritual, emotional, and physical needs, with enough left over to meet the needs of others around you. In this way, your life will be encompassed by the riches of His glory. God desires to bring us into this abundance of His goodness so we can share that abundance with others.

> ## TRUE ABUNDANCE IS GOD'S PROVISION FLOWING *TO* YOU SO THAT IT CAN FLOW *THROUGH* YOU.

ABUNDANCE IS A COMMAND: "BE FRUITFUL AND MULTIPLY"

To understand the full biblical picture of supernatural abundance, we need to identify when and where the principle of abundance was introduced on earth. We need to investigate God's purposes in creation:

> *Then God blessed* [Adam and Eve] *and said, "Be fruitful and multiply."* (Genesis 1:28 NLT)

Do you realize that the very first divine instruction given to humanity was all about manifesting abundance? *"Be fruitful and multiply"* was not just a suggestion—it was a command. God was speaking to Adam and Eve, our spiritual parents, and essentially telling them, "Whatever I've given to you has been given with the responsibility to recognize its importance and to steward it in the correct way, handling it carefully so it will continue to grow, increase, and expand. In this way, you'll never live in lack."

If you think this instruction was given to Adam and Eve alone, you only need to read the Scriptures a little further to discover that God spoke the same commandment again to Noah and his family in Genesis 8:17 and 9:1, 7 and to the Israelites in Leviticus 26:9.

When God says something once, we should listen. When He says something twice, we better get ready. But if God says something three or more times, we must realize that He's very serious about the matter—and it's time for us to listen and obey! God is very concerned about your well-being. His first priority is your spiritual wellness; but beyond that, He also desires for you to manifest abundance in the realms of your soul and body (see 3 John 1:2), "being fruitful and multiplying."

ABUNDANCE IS A GIFT: "POWER TO GET WEALTH"

The big picture continues as we move forward in God's relationship with the Israelites and see Him reminding His people that their power to gain wealth was supernatural—it came from Him and was directly related to His covenant with them:

> *And you shall remember the LORD your God, for it is He who gives you power to get wealth, that He may establish His covenant which He swore to your fathers, as it is this day.* (Deuteronomy 8:18 NKJV)

I love this Scripture passage from Deuteronomy because it teaches us the secret to being successful in all areas of life. Wealth is available to us. We just need to learn how to access it. I see this theme throughout the Scriptures. I call the process "manifesting abundance," and you may call it something else, but there is an entire realm of superabundance just waiting for you and me to explore it and put it to work. God wants to give you the power to gain wealth—in the fullest sense of that word. He wants to show you how to increase and multiply in many areas of your life. In these days, He is opening untapped realms of supernatural abundance to us. Why not jump into this glory flow!

ABUNDANCE IS ACCESSED THROUGH ABIDING AND RECEIVING

As we survey the unfolding scene of supernatural abundance that God reveals for us in His Word, we see that when we abide in God's presence, we can access His divine power to increase and multiply and gain wealth. As long as Adam and Eve remained in fellowship with God, they lived in the fullness of that abundance. As long as the Israelites stayed in right relationship with the Lord, they could receive the power to gain wealth in accordance with the covenant He had established with them. That is why He told them, *"You shall remember the LORD your God"* (Deuteronomy 8:18). But when Adam and Eve, and later the Israelites, moved away from their relationships with God, their ability to increase, multiply, and get wealth drastically diminished or disappeared.

In the New Testament, Jesus taught that we need to stay in the Vine or we won't be able to bear fruit:

Abide in Me, and I in you. As the branch cannot bear fruit of itself, except it abide in the vine; no more can you, except you abide in Me. I am the vine, you are the branches: He that abides in Me, and I in him, the same brings forth much fruit: for without Me you can do nothing.   (John 15:4–5)

Without an ongoing relationship with Jesus, without being in fellowship with the Father, we *"can do nothing,"* and this includes experiencing divine multiplication. But with Jesus, with the Father, all things are possible, including supernatural abundance! (See, for example, Mark 9:23.)

In the past, God has done a lot for all of us, but I believe that He is now releasing a very special impartation, a very special gift—a release of deeper understanding and operation of His love and care for us all. Far too often, we walk in the natural, or in what we can see and understand. Many people fear anything new, insisting on staying in the areas they are already familiar with. But God wants to catch us up into the wonder of His glory where we can begin to experience what we have never seen before and what has no human explanation. Then we will decree the things that God Himself has spoken to us. They won't have been spoken by any man or woman, but rather will have come directly from heaven. When we align ourselves with what God has spoken, suddenly, anything is possible. In God, there is no lack, loss, depletion, or decline. Rather, there is all-sufficiency. In the realms of His glory, there is a fullness of all things.

We enter into God's glory realm through our love, worship, faith, obedience, and service toward Him. As children of God, we can become bold and ask Him for supernatural miracles in areas where we have experienced difficulty or lack in the past. We can ask Him to invade our circumstances, to invade our life situations, and to reveal His glory in the midst of them. He is ready to do it. We just need to give Him permission to upset the daily routine of our lives and let His glory flow from heaven to earth. Then we need to take hold of our portion as it flows down from the throne. In those moments when His glory flows from heaven to earth, healing and other blessings can come to us in Jesus's mighty name.

As I emphasized previously, God's abundance can manifest in every area of our lives. For example, when doctors have spoken negative words, we can hold on to God's positive word that says, *"By His stripes we are healed"* (Isaiah 53:5 NKJV). And when we hold tight, healing will flow. If you need healing, just reach up into the spirit realm right now and pull down whatever it is you need. You must interact with the realm of glory. God won't force it on you. Pull it down. His healing is yours right now, in Jesus's mighty name. The miracle you have been needing is yours right now. Receive it.

You may need a miracle in your business. Just reach into the glory realm, grab hold of the miracle you need, and pull it down right now. Do it in Jesus's name.

"Is it all that easy?" some might ask.

Yes, it's just that easy. God's manifest abundance is there for you to access. Say, "What God has promised me belongs to me," and let it be yours.

You may need a miracle for your family, for a relationship, or for a difficult situation. Say to the Lord, "I am reaching up for what You have already provided for me, and I receive it now! You are wonderful, so I take hold of the fullness of Your wonder."

You may need to access the realms of God's glory for someone else's need. In the glory, you can receive an impartation for your family members, your friends, or others to whom the Lord sends you to minister. As you lift your hands into the realms of glory, those hands are being filled with healing power. There will be a transference of the healing anointing upon you. Reach up and take what you need and carry it to others. As we dare to access God's glory realms, He may perform creative miracles, such as restoring minds damaged by Alzheimer's and other forms of dementia. In exchange, He will offer us the most wonderful mind of all—the very mind of Christ.

If you stay in the Spirit long enough, your hands may actually begin to shimmer and glow with a golden glory. That golden glory speaks of the healings and miracles God will do through you in the days ahead. You will be receiving a new impartation of glory; and from that day on, God will bless the works of your hands. God is saying to you today, "Come all the way into My glory so that My glory may come all the way into you and begin to flow out through you."

Abide in Jesus. Stay in the glory. Receive God's abundant life for you and others.

Are you ready? Today, you must declare, "I am ready to move forward. I know I will not move in the same way I have moved in the past or do the same things I have been doing. I am ready for the 'new thing' God is doing in my life." (See Isaiah 43:19.)

THERE IS AN ENTIRE REALM OF SUPERABUNDANCE JUST WAITING FOR US TO EXPLORE IT AND PUT IT TO WORK.

ABUNDANCE COMES THROUGH SURRENDER

Living in the glory involves another foundational principle of abundance: we must surrender everything of ourselves to God in order to receive all that He has for us and all that He wants to pour out through us. When you offer your whole self to God as a *"living sacrifice"* (Romans 12:1), you become a channel for divine blessings to flow through your life to others. And, perhaps more than in any other way, God uses our hands to manifest and extend those blessings.

YIELDING YOUR HANDS

Let me ask you a question: where is God? Is He far off somewhere? Is He in some distant place? While His throne is in heaven, He is everywhere. (See, for example, Psalm 139:7–12.) But most wondrous of all, the moment we receive Christ, God lives inside us! (See John 14:23.) I am the "Joshua Mills" expression of Jesus Christ on the earth, and you are a unique expression of Jesus Christ too. If you believe God dwells inside you, and not just in heaven—and you're right, He does—then where are His hands? We must realize that He often uses *our* hands to minister to the world. As you surrender to Him in the glory, your hands become the very hands of God, reaching out to bless others. You were created to live in the glory realm, and God wants to release His glory and abundance through you to many other people.

God's creative glory resides within you through His Spirit, and He will release that creative glory through your hands. Let's take this point a step further. We know that God has said He has given us the power to get wealth. (See Deuteronomy 8:18; Ecclesiastes 5:19.) If you receive that power, you will begin to do things you've never done before. Your hands will become supernatural portals for God's power to flow out through you, releasing divine creativity connected with receiving abundance in all spheres of life.

In my experience, creative direction from heaven can come to you as clear as a map to follow. Take hold of it. It has the answers to questions you've been asking. It contains clear solutions for problems you've been facing.

Not long ago, during a seven-city ministry tour, I was ministering in Tulsa, Oklahoma. One night, as I stood behind the pulpit, I was somewhat surprised to see a very tall angel directly in front of me. The other people in attendance couldn't see him—although both pastors who were present later mentioned to me that they were aware of an angelic presence. However, I could see this angel strongly in my spirit. He was dressed in white, luminescent garments. I had seen many angels appear in this way before, but what really struck me about his presence and surprised me was the object he was holding.

In his hands, he held a large, long scroll that had an ancient appearance to it. He opened it, and I could see that it was a map of directions. Although I couldn't quite decipher all the details on this map, I instantly knew in my spirit that God was showing me the future path He had already prepared for me, my family, and our ministry. This map was being supernaturally downloaded to me. God was bringing me spiritual and natural clarity for the journey ahead. This revelation brought great encouragement to my spirit.

Later that evening, I shared these details with Janet. The next day, while we were driving to Texas, we were both shocked when we called one of our spiritual mentors, Momma Billie Deck, because, without any knowledge of what had happened the night before, she said, "I see God giving you a map of directions. He's downloading it to your spirit. He's making a way." Yes! That is exactly what He was doing for us—and I believe He's doing the same for you right now, even as you read this book. You might not see a vision of a scroll, but God is birthing something in your spirit. Reach up and take it. Say, "Yes, Lord!"

I'm talking about your receiving new inventions, new blueprints, new patterns. God will release heavenly "scrolls" with instructions for you and others to follow. Take hold of those supernatural instructions and run with them, and you will surely prosper.

This touch from heaven enables you to do what you have long known you were called to do but couldn't accomplish in your own ability. God Himself will unfold revelation after revelation to you, enabling you to know and understand what you have never known or understood before. This will allow you to step through new doors that will open for you. To others, the results will be unexplainable.

PURIFYING YOUR HANDS

I want you to truly recognize that your hands were made for creative glory—for blessing and abundance. These days, our hands do a lot of "speaking." I don't just mean through sign language. I'm talking about using our hands to text, to email, or to type on a tablet or laptop. Such practices are part of our modern society, and God is about to revolutionize what comes forth from your hands through these avenues and in many other ways. But for this to happen, our hands need to be purified, spiritually speaking. This enables us to stay in the glory.

> Who shall ascend into the hill of the LORD? or who shall stand in His holy place? He that has clean hands, and a pure heart; who has not lifted up his soul to vanity, nor sworn deceitfully. (Psalm 24:3–4)

Your hands were not created for *taking* nearly as much as they were created for *giving out*. Too often, taking involves a violation, leaving someone else with loss. Your hands were not made for greed. God didn't create you just to take from others. Your hands were made for giving!

Even the receiving we do with our hands is creatively abundant if we are in the glory. When we receive from God or other people what the Lord has established for us to receive, we don't leave Him or His servants with loss. In such a situation, what others extend to us is what God has ordained for our lives all along. Therefore, when you receive from the hands of others, you make a way for their blessing as well.

Needless to say, when we give, we make a way for our own blessing too. May the Lord use our hands in greater and greater ways to give, to bless, and even to receive.

YOUR HANDS ARE MADE FOR CREATIVE GLORY, MADE FOR BLESSING OTHERS.

In the days ahead, may we be taught by the Spirit to use our hands for His purposes. May God show us the areas where we have sinned with our hands so that we may determine not to do it again. Let our hands be holy, consecrated, and totally dedicated to the Lord and His work so that He will receive all the glory.

Sometimes, our portals to the spirit realm become blocked. We plug up the power that would normally move through us, stopping the flow. This can happen when we've had too much junk in relation to our hands for the healing flow to come forth. If that is the case with you, I'm not saying you have to do something so that God will love you more and therefore use you more. He already loves you as much as He could ever love you. But if you have sinned, you do need to be restored to Him, and you can be.

Do you believe that God is your Redeemer? Do you believe that He is your Restorer? Do you believe that He forgives you when you have made a mistake? I hope you do. These are all fruits of His great love. When, by faith, you grab hold of God's Word, receiving His forgiveness and restoration, it opens your blocked portals and lets the glory flow freely again. God's power can flow into you, and it can also flow out through you.

When we dedicate our hands to God's purposes, not only can creative ideas come, but supernatural wonders can also happen. Jesus said we would lay hands on the sick, and they would recover. (See Mark 16:18.) This will not occur because of what we are able to do, but because we have made way for the Spirit of God to flow through us. We must make a way for His abundance to flow.

ABUNDANCE IS ACTIVATED BY FAITH

God's Spirit is inviting us to step into His realm of superabundance and enjoy its benefits, but as I said earlier, He will not force us to do so. We must determine, we must choose, to move into what God is offering us. Too many well-meaning Christians have said, "Well, if God wants me to have it, He'll bring it to me." Yes, God is sovereign, and there are moments in our lives when, in our inability to perceive, He shows up with His divine presence and brings us blessings, brings us abundance, brings us miracles, brings us breakthroughs. But the Bible declares in no uncertain terms that *"the righteous will live by faith"* (Romans 1:17 NIV). God can do it all, but He is looking for men and women who will rise up in faith and choose to move forward into every promise He has given. We may think we are waiting for Him to move, but He is often waiting for us to move in faith toward His promises!

Faith is not found just in the words we read or speak. Faith requires action, and faith produces action. When true faith is established in our hearts, we can no longer do the limiting, unproductive, even damaging things we used to do. Instead, we are given to doing the positive, fruitful, uplifting things that our faith dictates. We are given to living abundantly.

ABUNDANCE IS INITIATED BY SOWING

One of the primary actions of faith is "sowing." Galatians 6:7 delivers this powerful truth: *"Do not be deceived, God is not mocked; for whatever a man sows, that he will also reap"* (NKJV).

It is easy to be deceived about the nature and role of God's abundance in our lives. The human mind is easily twisted. But supernatural abundance is something we cannot afford to be deceived about. Some people have the mistaken idea that the principle of sowing and reaping was only for another time in history and does not hold any real meaning for us as believers today. Well, to that, I say, "Look at the natural world, which often reflects the spiritual world: we still have farmers. Without them, we wouldn't have food to eat. Tell any farmer that you no longer believe in sowing and reaping, and they will be quick to reply that this principle does not only apply to some other era. It is actually very relevant today—in both the physical and spiritual realms. In fact, the principle of sowing and reaping is eternal."

A farmer who didn't believe in sowing and reaping would quickly go bankrupt. Moreover, every farmer knows that the specific seeds they sow in the ground will yield fully grown plants of the same type they have sowed. If the farmer wants to harvest pumpkins, he doesn't plant apple seeds but pumpkin seeds. We often lose sight of this reality in our spiritual lives (and even often in our natural lives): whatever we sow is what we will reap.

Some well-meaning Christians keep praying and praying, asking God why He doesn't seem to be moving in their finances, why He is not bringing them into abundance and increase. Why should He? They are reaping what they have sowed, and they have not been sowing financially. It is not enough to sow seeds of love or kindness and expect them to bring in a financial harvest, although that might happen at times. (See, for example, 1 Timothy 5:17–18.) A financial harvest will come from sowing financial seeds. A solid financial investment brings a good financial return.

I couldn't tell you this principle if I had not first practiced it myself in all areas of my life. I can affirm that what I am describing is not merely a theory or an idea that I heard someone else talking about. This is a principle that God has been teaching me since I was a teenager. When a miracle seed is deposited into miracle soil, it produces a miracle harvest in the life of the one who has sowed it.

It is time for you to begin sowing some miracle seeds and expecting a miracle harvest. We will talk more about how to do this as the book progresses. Sow into the soil of God's glory, and He will send you a glory harvest!

> *Whoever sows to please their flesh, from the flesh will reap destruction; whoever sows to please the Spirit, from the Spirit will reap eternal life. Let us not become weary in doing good, for at the proper time we will reap a harvest if we do not give up [*"do not lose heart"* NKJV].* (Galatians 6:8–9 NIV)

Whatever we do, we cannot lose heart. We cannot grow weary in doing good. What does this mean? It refers to persevering during the interval between the sowing of the seed and the reaping of the harvest. In the natural, the period of time between the planting in the spring and the harvesting in the fall is called *summer*. During a spiritual summertime, some people begin to wonder if anything is happening. I want to assure you that if you have done what God has spoken to you to do, you can know that He will accomplish what He has said He will do. If your seed has been placed in fertile soil, never doubt that your harvest is coming. Oh, it's coming!

WHEN A MIRACLE SEED IS DEPOSITED INTO MIRACLE SOIL, IT PRODUCES A MIRACLE HARVEST.

ABUNDANCE IS CONTINGENT UPON HONORING THE LORD

The big picture of living in God's abundance also includes the understanding that we are to honor Him first with our wealth. Abundance is not all about us—it is about God's glory!

Let's look at two additional Scriptures that describe the abundant fruitfulness that God wants for us. The first is from the prophet Joel, who declared,

> *And the floors shall be full of wheat, and the vats shall overflow with wine and oil.* (Joel 2:24)

I invite you to personalize this promise and say it this way: "*My* floors shall be full of wheat, and *my* vats shall overflow with wine and oil."

God gives us His spiritual wine to fill our hearts with joy, and He gives us His anointing oil to make our faces shine. He is changing our countenances, making us the happiest of people as we rejoice in His presence and in His daily provision for us.

Second, the wise King Solomon wrote, "*So shall your storage places* ["barns" NKJV] *be filled with plenty, and your vats shall be overflowing with new wine*" (Proverbs 3:10 AMPC).

Let's personalize this verse as well: "*My* storage places shall be filled with plenty, and *my* vats shall overflow with new wine."

The passage in Proverbs where this verse is found comes with both a revelation and an instruction. Let's read the verse that comes before it: "*Honor the Lord with your capital and sufficiency [from righteous labors] and with the firstfruits of all your income*" (Proverbs 3:9 AMPC). The *New Living Translation* says it this way: "*Honor the* LORD *with your wealth and with the best part of everything you produce.*"

What follows this act of honoring—full barns (representing storage places) and overflowing vats (representing containers such as bank accounts, wallets, or other items in which you hold abundance)—are the results of our obedience to the divine instruction.

How do we get to this place of abundance where we are filled and overflowing? Like most twenty-first century citizens of earth, we all want the plenty that this passage speaks of. We love the images of filled barns and overflowing vats. We welcome the wine and the oil. However, we often neglect to look more closely to see how this can be achieved. We frequently ignore the simple instruction that precedes it—and the two go together. You can't have the one without the other.

The Scriptures are very clear on this point. The revelation is there for anyone who cares to seek it out. In faith, you can honor God with your wealth, and you should. And when you do, He will reward you bountifully.

At times, when I am preaching and say something like this, the room suddenly gets very quiet. In general, in modern society, speaking about money is taboo. It's considered a private matter, and many people would rather not speak about it openly. Yet Jesus didn't have this outlook. He spoke very openly about money. In fact, He had a lot to say about finances. His teachings help us to understand that, in the hands of the right people, money can be a divine supernatural tool. Who are these right people? Those who choose to align themselves with God's purposes.

MONEY AND OUR HANDS

Previously, I mentioned dedicating our hands to the Lord. Our prayers concerning our hands must include the way we use our money. Now, don't get me wrong. Abundance is not all about money. Actually, it's mostly *not* about money, but how we handle our finances affects everything else in our lives.

For most of us, our hands and our money go together. We count our money with our hands. We take our debit card out and put it away with our hands. We write out checks with our hands. We use our hands to type on our smart phones or computers for online access to our bank statements and other records, to transfer funds to or from certain accounts, and to pay bills.

HOW WE HANDLE OUR FINANCES AFFECTS EVERYTHING ELSE IN OUR LIVES.

In the past, we may have used our money in ways that were not pleasing to God, ways that did not honor Him. I don't know about you, but I want to honor the Lord in everything I do!

For example, have you ever wanted to buy something for yourself, and while you were in the process of making that purchase, you realized that you shouldn't do it? That's not to say that what you were buying was bad. Still, you knew you shouldn't be buying it. The Holy Spirit within you was saying, "Stop!"

There might be various reasons why the Spirit would warn you in this way. For instance, perhaps He knew you would fall into difficulty if you bought the item because you would be financially overextending yourself. If you couldn't pay your bills, it might affect your credit rating. If the Holy Spirit has told you He doesn't want you to go into debt, and you are charging whatever it is you want to buy, without being able to pay it off in full by the end of the monthly credit cycle, you are headed for trouble.

"Don't buy that," you sense the Spirit saying.

"But I really like it," your flesh replies. "There is nothing wrong with this. How could it be wrong?"

It's a good question. The answer is this: anything that goes against the voice of the Holy Spirit is sin. I know that might be a difficult pill for some people to swallow, but it's the truth. If you do or buy anything that goes against the voice of the Holy Spirit, you are living in disobedience. (See Ephesians 4:30.)

Surely, you would not want to live in disobedience to God. So, these are important issues.

I'm not just writing this for your benefit. I am speaking to myself as well. There have been times when I wanted something very badly, but I didn't have the money to buy it, so I thought, "Well, I can just pay for it with a credit card. After all, there's nothing wrong with it. It will be a blessing to others. It will be a blessing to my own family." And yet the Spirit was saying, "Don't do it. You don't need that. Don't buy it."

God knows what is best for you, so ask Him. Then, after He has spoken, obey what He says. He wants you to use your hands for righteousness and not for disobedience. And He has given you the ability to resist temptation (see 1 Corinthians 10:13) and to bring every thought captive to the obedience of Christ (see 2 Corinthians 10:5). God also gives you authority over every evil spirit, including the "spirit of mammon"—any demonic influence that would prompt you to elevate money to the place of God in your life. (See Matthew 6:24.)

Whenever money comes into our hands, we need to consult the Lord about what we are to do with it—and then do what we know is right. Asking God about using our money wisely is one of the ways we learn to hear His voice and obey His Spirit. It's also one of the ways we begin experiencing divine abundance.

PRIORITIZING OUR FINANCES

My friend Ryan Rufus of New Nature Ministries wrote a blog in which he offered some very sound advice concerning the godly stewardship of our finances. It shows us how to honor the Lord with our wealth. Here is an excerpt from that blog:

> There are seven things that demand your money with every paycheck, and it is vital how you prioritize each one. Which should I pay first? Which should I pay last? How do I order everything in between?
>
> This is how you should steward each paycheck. Each one is listed in order of priority:
>
> 1. Tithe/give/sow
>
> 2. Tax
>
> 3. Debt
>
> 4. Save
>
> 5. Bills
>
> 6. Necessities
>
> 7. Luxuries
>
> If you divide up every paycheck into these seven areas and prioritize them in this order, you will eventually get out of debt and into abundance. This is how my wife and I order our finances, and it works! It may not work straightaway, but give it time and stick to it, and it will eventually start working for you.
>
> The first four things should be done before you even spend a cent on anything else. Luxuries must absolutely always come last. This is essential. Only buy luxuries once you've taken care of all the other things and only if you have money left over. NEVER go into debt for luxuries!
>
> Here is the problem, though: people often put luxuries first.... In fact, a lot of people order their spending in the exact opposite way than they should be doing, and their financial priority list ends up looking like this:

1. Luxuries

2. Necessities

3. Bills

4. Savings

5. Debts

6. Tax

7. Tithe/give/sow

The problem when you order it this way is that there is usually no money left after number 3, which means there's no chance of saving or paying debts or taxes—and giving to God is just impossible. If giving is last on your list, and you do somehow manage to have a little bit left at this point, can you imagine how hard it will be to give it?

The solution is so simple. Flip your budget over!

1. Give first. Put God first in your finances. This is the point where it's the easiest to give; but the longer you leave it, the harder it gets.

2. Tax. Put a little money aside from every paycheck into a separate account so it's there at tax time.

3. Debts. Put as much money as you can every paycheck toward paying off your debts so you can get rid of them as quickly as possible and not be overwhelmed by interest. Once your debts are cleared, your savings are going to rocket.

4. Save. Try to put some money aside in a savings account every paycheck, even a small amount. Over a few years, this adds up. And then spend savings mostly on assets rather than on liabilities. (Research the difference.)

5. Bills. Pay your bills as soon as you can, and try to limit them so you can free up money for savings and unexpected expenses.

6. Necessities. Know the difference between a necessity and a luxury. The problem is that people often convince themselves that luxuries are necessities. Food, transportation, accommodation, medication, and basic clothing are necessities. Eating out at restaurants, buying new things, upgrading technology, vacations, and entertainment are all luxuries we crave—not absolute necessities.

7. Luxuries. There's nothing wrong with luxuries, but keep them last on the priority list.[2]

Again, to the righteous, money is a supernatural and strategic tool that can cause the kingdom of God to move forward and expand. But when placed in the hands of the wrong people, money is a dangerous weapon for the acceleration of the kingdom of darkness. I'm not just referring to money in the hands of "sinners." The same is true for money in the hands of believers who are not listening to the voice of the Spirit. That money can become a curse instead of the blessing God intended it to be.

Obeying the instructions in Proverbs 3:9, *"Honor the Lord with your wealth and with the best part of everything you produce"* (NLT), can mean all the difference in our lives. I need to honor the Lord with my finances, and you do too. This is a key principle. It is a major revelation of abundance. This is the Spirit's instruction: *"Honor the Lord."*

We must honor the voice of the Holy Spirit, who lives within us and speaks to us so clearly every single day if we listen and discern His voice. If we honor that voice and honor the Lord through our finances, then the Bible says, *"So shall your storage places ["barns" NKJV] be filled with plenty, and your vats shall be overflowing with new wine"* (Proverbs 3:10 AMPC). Hallelujah!

It's so simple. God says, "Honor Me, and if you do, good things will happen for you." He desires for you to live a generous lifestyle. Why? Because this positions you to receive the generous blessings of heaven.

---

2. Ryan Rufus, "How to Steward Each Paycheck to Get out of Debt and into Abundance," September 1, 2018, https://www.newnatureministries.org/blog-post/how-to-steward-each-paycheck-to-get-out-of-debt-and-into-abundance/. Used by permission and edited for this publication.

ABUNDANCE AND TRUE WORSHIP GO TOGETHER

The last (but certainly not least!) foundational biblical principle of abundance is that the true worship of God and increase go together. Whenever you honor the Lord, aligning yourself with Him and His purposes, living in His presence through heartfelt worship and a yielded heart, you can't help but be blessed. Worship leads you into the abundance of God's heart.

WORSHIP IN SPIRIT AND TRUTH

Jesus made it very clear to the Samaritan woman that the Father is looking for those who will worship Him *"in spirit and in truth."* (See John 4:23–24.) You cannot worship in truth unless you're worshipping in spirit because anything else is a false reality. When you worship in spirit, it's because you have received a revelation from God concerning worship and its power to change your life and circumstances.

Worshipping Him in spirit and truth will cause you to begin to feel His joy, His goodness, and His glory; then, in the midst of that glory, you will encounter the angels of heaven gathering to join you. This is because when you honor the Lord and move yourself into alignment with Him through worship, the angels are there to worship with you.

If you sing, "Holy, holy, holy," you will join the song of heaven, which the angels are already singing (see, for example, Revelation 4:8), and you will find yourself encountering God in a new way. Your praise and worship will create a pathway for you to travel into God's divine presence. If you dance before the Lord, the angels will join in. Soon, Ezekiel's "wheel within a wheel" will be turning (see Ezekiel 1:16), and God will turn some negative things around for you.

Similarly, if you honor the Lord with your finances, if you honor the voice of the Holy Spirit in regard to the giving of your wealth, you will discover that there are angels of abundance moving in that supernatural realm, blessing you—and you will find that your giving has become a bridge for you to travel into the depths of God's goodness and supernatural provision.

Again, this Scripture from Proverbs 3 provides us with great revelation concerning our finances and the way we can honor the Lord with our wealth through the correct stewardship of the bountiful provisions He has brought into our lives:

> *Honor the LORD with your wealth and with the best part of everything you produce. Then he will fill your barns with grain, and your vats will overflow with good wine.* (Proverbs 3:9–10 NLT)

A MULTIMILLION-DOLLAR TESTIMONY

My dear friends Tony and Sandy Krishack are the pastors of Victory Christian Center, a wonderful Foursquare church in Houston, Texas. I've had the privilege of ministering at their church every year for more than fifteen years. Several years ago, the Lord spoke to Pastor Tony from Proverbs 3:9–10 and challenged him to obey it fully and to encourage his people to do the same and see what would happen. Pastor Tony was faithful to the vision and began encouraging his people to honor the Lord with their wealth.

He laid it all out before them in a simple way: First, there is the "stuff" we already have. This includes the blessings God has caused to come to us. Second, there is the promise: if we do the right thing with what we have, our barns will be filled with plenty and our vats will be bursting with wine. That's the "stuff" we will receive. God is just waiting for us to release what we have so that He can bring us into the greater things He has promised.

Every Sunday, when Pastor Tony stood to receive the offering, just as the Lord had spoken to him, he shared Proverbs 3:9–10, encouraging the people to give of what they had in order to obtain what God had available for them, to give of their current "stuff" so they could receive all that He had promised. As you can imagine, things began to change for the better in the lives of the members of Victory Christian Center.

Each week, Pastor Tony invited people to come forward and testify about what they were experiencing. "I don't want to know what your salary is or how much money you're making on your job," he told them. "I don't want to know about any government checks you normally receive. What I'm interested in is the increase, the overflow, the abundance that comes to you. If you experience a supernatural debt reduction, I want to know about that. If you receive an unexpected bonus at your job or an unexpected increase in salary, I want to know about it. If you have money come in unexpectedly from any unusual source, I want to know about it."

Weekly, the testimonies began to come in, and Pastor Tony, who is a very organized person, wrote them all down. I love that about him. Even though he is open to moving in the Spirit, he is also an excellent administrator who does things in an orderly way. From the first day, he has kept track of the miracles and the abundance that have come to the members of that church since they entered into the revelation of Proverbs 3:9–10 and began obeying its instructions.

In the first three years and eleven months, those increases amounted to twenty-six million dollars. Is Victory Christian Center a megachurch with many thousands of members? No, it is a congregation of about four hundred people. Yet, together, they have received twenty-six million dollars in increases from the Lord. Why did this happen? Because they heard what God was saying, and they believed it and obeyed it. Honoring God, honoring the voice of the Spirit and being led by His voice, is the greatest key to entering into the unlimited abundance He has prepared for those of us who love Him and want to do His will.

ARE YOU READY TO RECEIVE?

In this chapter, we have looked at the "biblical big picture" of God's abundance for us, setting the scene and laying the foundation for the rest of this book. Again, we need these establishing principles to be able to fully understand and apply the seven divine mysteries.

At the end of each divine mystery chapter, I have included prophetic decrees that will help you to put into action the faith that will build within you as you read about the specific mysteries. You will be enabled to make these decrees with complete confidence, knowing that God watches over His Word to perform it in your life. (See Jeremiah 1:12 AMP.) As you speak the decrees, you may feel that some of the statements resonate with you more strongly than others. This is okay. God is establishing His truth within you. Write down the ones that you feel most confident about and place them on a mirror, refrigerator door, bulletin board, or anywhere else where you will see them often. These notes will remind you to speak the decrees on a daily basis.

If you want to move into a new realm of unlimited abundance in God, I encourage you to read on and to keep your heart open. Jesus said, *"I came that they may have and enjoy life, and have it in abundance [to the full, till it overflows]"* (John 10:10 AMP). He was talking about you.

There is not a single area of your life for which God does not have a promise of victory. There is not one situation that you face for which God has not already established a way of overcoming for you in His Word. His abundance is at your disposal. Are you ready to learn how to receive it?

Prepare to unlock all *7 Divine Mysteries* as you begin manifesting unlimited abundance in every area of your life!

CHAPTER 2

DIVINE MYSTERY #1: HEAVENLY VISION IS A PATHWAY FOR PROVISION

"Beloved, I pray that in every way you may succeed and prosper
and be in good health [physically],
just as [I know] your soul prospers [spiritually]."
—3 John 1:2 (AMP)

We are living in a time of terrible fear, a time when falsehoods and rumors spread quickly and take hold of large numbers of people. It is amazing how total fabrications become accepted by so many in such a short time. Satan, whom I call the "enemy spirit," is truly the father of lies (see John 8:44), and he is attempting to invade our minds with all kinds of lies and wickedness. This requires that we no longer walk by our natural insight. We must operate by the Spirit.

If you focus on natural problems long enough, things will look so bad that you could easily become discouraged. Rather, look to God and be led onto the pathway of provision illuminated by His Spirit. The Bible says, *"Where there is no vision, the people perish"* (Proverbs 29:18 KJV). In this day, we must receive heavenly vision; when we do, instead of perishing, we will begin prospering. The true sons and daughters of God are those who are Spirit-led. (See Romans 8:14.)

In the midst of all of the chaos, God has been giving me new revelation that can take us to another level. One night, when I was at home, revelation was being downloaded into my spirit so powerfully that, about midnight, I jumped up from the kitchen table where I was working and started praising God in tongues and dancing around the house. Suddenly I *knew* this truth: *heavenly vision is a pathway for provision.* Let this revelation invade your heart as well. God's abundance is available as we receive a vision from Him concerning His all-sufficient provision for us. In this chapter, I want to explore several Scriptures that, combined, will give you a heavenly vision of abundance for your life.

REALIZE THIS: "DANGER WILL NOT COME NEAR YOU"

God said, *"A thousand may fall at your side and ten thousand at your right hand, but it* ["danger" AMP] *will not come near you"* (Psalm 91:7).

Take this word as your own and let it be established in your heart as part of God's heavenly vision for you. Say, "Danger will not come near me." That means:

- Anything that endangers your health and wellness is not permitted.
- Anything that endangers your family and healthy relationships is not permitted.
- Anything that endangers your financial well-being is not permitted.
- Anything that endangers your peace of mind is not permitted.
- Anything that endangers your spiritual growth and success is not permitted.

Say it again, out loud:

"Danger will not come near me."

That's what God said, and that's the way you need to talk as well. Too many beautiful, God-fearing believers are accepting the terminology of the world around them and not holding on to what God is saying. I don't doubt the fact that they may love Jesus with all of their hearts, but the way they talk is destructive, pulling them away from God's purposes for them. Instead of speaking God's words, they speak words of fear and hopelessness.

I find that I have to correct some believers for talking in this way. "You shouldn't say that," I tell them. "That's not what God has said. Instead, *this* is God's promise: 'Danger will not come near you.' You must come into agreement with Him and speak what He has spoken."

Jesus said that the enemy *"has only one thing in mind—he wants to steal, slaughter, and destroy"* (John 10:10 TPT). You can break the curses of the enemy by standing with God and His Word. Stop coming into agreement with the curses and start coming into agreement with God's blessings. Make up your mind to cease conforming to the words of the enemy, and then declare, "I am determined to come out of agreement with every curse that has been spoken over me. Therefore, I turn and come into agreement with the blessings of heaven that God has spoken over my life." It works!

In Psalm 91:9–10, the psalmist says, *"Because you have made the* LORD, *[who is] my refuge, even the Most High, your dwelling place, no evil will befall you, nor will any plague come near your tent"* (AMP).

Why will no evil befall us nor any plague come near our tents? Because we have made the Lord, who is our refuge, even the Most High, our dwelling place. This is the word that we need to live by, not the word of the world. Do you live in that place? What place am I referring to? The secret place, the dwelling of God, the glory realm. Make His secret place your home.

What is the promise again? *"No evil will befall you."* I encourage you to say it now:

"No evil will befall me."

You need to capture that thought and declare, "This is mine—right now. No evil will befall me. It might try, but it won't succeed."

"Nor will any plague come near your tent." Affirm this promise as well:

"No plague will come near my tent."

When Psalm 91 was written, many people lived in tents. You might live in an apartment, a townhouse, a condo, a single-family home, or a mansion. Someone who is reading this book might even live in a cave. I don't know where you reside, but I do know God and His promises, so I can say, without hesitation, that wherever you live, I want you to take this word to heart and stand on it, declaring, "No plague will come near my home. No plague will come near where I live—including the plagues of lack and insufficiency. When others complain about this world being 'plagued with problems,' I will continue to trust God's Word, which promises an abundant overflow of provision."

The Lord has taught me to live in His glory realm. This is an atmosphere, a place, that few might understand. I am living in the glory, and the glory is living in me. Glory realm realities have become my heavenly vision; in turn, this vision has opened to me an unlimited realm of abundance. The beautiful thing about having a vision is that it keeps you moving forward. When you're in motion, you're moving away from one thing and toward another. When God gives us a vision of His abundance, it moves us away from lack and toward His overflow. The vision unravels the mystery of how to maintain our journey on the pathway of abundance God designed for us before we were born.

WHEN GOD GIVES US A VISION OF HIS ABUNDANCE, IT MOVES US AWAY FROM LACK AND TOWARD HIS OVERFLOW.

The next verses in Psalm 91 are powerful as well:

*For **He will** command His angels in regard to you, to protect and defend and guard you in all your ways [of obedience and service]. **They will** lift you up in their hands, so that you do not [even] strike your foot against a stone.* (Psalm 91:11–12 AMP)

"For He will...." Who will? God will. What will God do? *"He will command His angels...."* Whose angels are being referred to? These are God's angels. *"He will command His angels in regard to **you**."* I'm so glad that God made that point personal. The angels will not serve just anyone—they are sent to serve those who have made the Most High their dwelling place. Therefore, we are not wrong to call them "our" angels as well. God is giving us a gift: angels to attend to our every need—to *your* personal needs.

God has many gifts for us, and they all begin with the wonderful gift of salvation through Jesus Christ. When we come into that salvation experience, however, that's not the end of our journey. That's just the beginning of walking with the Lord. When we learn to walk with Him and capture His divine vision for our lives, the reality that we walk in is much different from the reality we have known in the world. There is no comparison. And one of the differences is the presence of angels attending to our every need, as described above. They come to guard, protect, and defend us, and they will do much more as we learn to interact with them and put them to work on our behalf. We will look at their role in greater detail in chapter 7, "Divine Mystery #6: Angel Power Makes Abundance Shower."

RECOGNIZE GOD'S PLANS TO PROSPER YOU

God has a plan for your life, and it's a wonderful one. That's good news because too often we don't even know what's going on in our lives! Thank God that He cares so much for us and has made provision for us in every way:

> *"For I know the plans I have for you,"* declares the LORD, *"plans to prosper you and not to harm you, plans to give you hope and a future."*   (Jeremiah 29:11 NIV)

God's plan is for us to prosper, and when we get on board with His plan, we *will* prosper. But, again, we must first see His vision for our lives. This involves replacing our limited perspectives about abundance.

What do you think of when you hear the word *abundance*? What's the first idea that comes to your mind? Perhaps *overflow*? That's a good word. I love it when my blessings are overflowing. The psalmist David said, *"My cup overflows"* (Psalm 23:5 NIV; AMP; NLT; TPT). He understood God's overflowing abundance.

When I consider abundance, I think of unlimited supply in every way: My heart being filled with unlimited love. My mind being filled with unlimited creativity and wisdom. My family members being filled with unlimited peace. My relationships being filled with unlimited kindness. My bank accounts overflowing with an unlimited financial supply.

When I refer to "unlimited supply," I'm not talking about just being able to pay my bills. I'm not talking about meeting my obligations and having a little left over. I'm talking about a bank account with sizeable funds. I'm talking about so much money that you will have to get on your knees and pray to seek God's guidance about where to direct this increase. You might soon be praying, "What am I to do with all this money, Lord?" Wouldn't that be a wonderful problem to have!

Whenever I discuss money, a great number of Christians tune me out. Some have told me, "Joshua, Jesus didn't die on the cross so that I could have more money; He died so that I could have salvation." And that is absolutely true. Jesus died for the salvation of our souls so that we could be prosperous in our spirits. Yet I have discovered this principle: what begins in my spirit doesn't stay in my spirit. It affects every part of my life.

Some people try to compartmentalize their faith. On Sunday, or when they're with the pastor or a visiting evangelist, they think and act in a certain way. Then, from Monday to Saturday, they think and act very differently. They behave one way at church and a very different way at work. Why do they do this? They lack a heavenly vision that permeates their lives.

With passion, the apostle John wrote to the early church:

> *Beloved, I pray that **in every way you may succeed and prosper**
> and be in good health [physically], just as [I know] your soul prospers
> [spiritually].*   (3 John 1:2 AMP)

In this verse, prosperity is connected to the health of your body and the health of your soul, and it means just what it says. If you think that God wants you to be sick, you're wrong. He doesn't. He has a better plan for you.

If you're battling sickness, I'm not condemning you—I'm giving you hope and, through the Spirit, opening a doorway for your healing. Step through. God wants you to prosper and be in good health, even as your soul prospers. The soul refers to your mind, your will, and your emotions. John was speaking about spiritual prosperity, soulish prosperity, and also physical prosperity. God wants you to prosper in all aspects of your life.

Why, then, do some people have a problem with financial prosperity? If God wants this for us, what's the issue?

Granted, prosperity does not begin with our finances. It begins with our spirits, the eternal part of us. That is what is saved. But if the Spirit wants us to prosper in every way, then we are to go beyond spiritual prosperity. Remember, God has a plan for your life, and prosperity is part of that plan. His purpose includes overflowing abundance. If you don't think God wants to prosper you, it's time to read your Bible again. Jesus came to redeem you completely.

HAVE AN ABUNDANCE MINDSET

I believe that God wants to change your mindset about abundance—the way that you have understood or misunderstood the abundant life. Of course, our life in God begins by knowing Christ as our personal Savior, and this begins in our spirit. But, at some point, our spiritual transformation must begin to transform our minds and the way we think about *everything*. The fact that you're reading this book proves that you have a deep spiritual desire to grow in the Spirit—and that supernatural hunger is what will open your mind to greater possibilities in God. If you want to live in divine abundance, you must have an abundance mindset. Small thinking will limit you, but abundance thinking will cause you to flourish and grow…grow…GROW!

I've discovered that one of the ways the Spirit can enlarge our capacity to *receive* abundantly is by challenging our capacity to *release* abundantly. Not long ago, as Janet and I were caught up in the presence of God during a Sunday morning church service, I had a strong desire to sow a significant financial seed into the glory realm. As I was preparing my offering, Janet leaned over to me and said, "Let's double our seed!" Although the original amount was already what I would consider to be an abundant gift, I was excited to double it according to Janet's faith, in anticipation of what the Spirit was preparing to do. Whenever God asks you to sow a seed, He already has your harvest in mind. He's simply looking for those who are obedient to do what He asks, in order to pour out abundance in overflow! We sowed our seed into the glory realm—and within minutes, we reaped a harvest! I know that sounds too good to be true, but *it is true*! Shortly afterward, we were presented with an unexpected check for double the amount that we had sowed! Wow! It was a magnificent harvest. And that is the way abundance works. God wants to give us an abundance mindset so that we can receive abundantly from Him.

Once, while ministering in Pensacola, Florida, I offered those present an opportunity to sow into the glory realm. A woman named Victoria sowed a sacrificial seed of $20 into the glory. Please note that the amount of the seed is between you and the Spirit, but it's important to learn how to allow Him to cause generosity to rise within your heart. Some people may sow twenty dollars, while others may be challenged to sow one hundred dollars, five hundred dollars, or thousands of dollars. Just a day later, we received a testimony from Victoria that she had received an unexpected gift of $1,000 in cash in an envelope. That was *fifty times* more than she had sowed. She recognized that the harvest had come in response to her seed. The nighttime seed had produced a next-day harvest! And this is the way it works in the glory realms. There is acceleration upon the growth of our seed when we choose to sow into the glory. A few days later, we received another report from Victoria: "The testimony of increase and abundance continues…. We received another $1,000 yesterday!" Now, that was *one hundred times* more than the seed that was initially sown. The Bible speaks to us about harvests of thirty, sixty, and one hundred times what was planted (see, for example, Mark 4:20), but even more than that, Deuteronomy 1:11 says, *"May the Lord…multiply you a thousand times more and bless you as he promised!"* (NLT). Allow the Spirit to stretch your mind with His greater possibilities! There are new realms of abundance to discover, but it's going to require our willingness to receive an abundance mindset and our dedication to walking in obedience to the Spirit's instructions.

When I consider the idea of abundance, I also think of gold and silver, which is very biblical. God said, *"The silver is Mine and the gold is Mine"* (Haggai 2:8 AMP). Again, God doesn't have a problem talking about money. He said it was all His, and since we are His, that means we share in all that He has. I don't know about you, but I want to accept the fullness of God's plan! His way is best.

> GOD'S PLAN IS FOR US TO PROSPER,
> AND WHEN WE GET ON BOARD WITH HIS PLAN,
> WE *WILL* PROSPER.

PICTURE A THANKSGIVING FEAST!

The topic of abundance also makes me think of a wonderful Thanksgiving dinner with all the trimmings. Each year, my family celebrates the holiday at my sister Katie's house, where there is always plenty of turkey. We eat so much turkey that we have to sleep it off. Every time, it seems like there are more sweet potatoes and delicious bread stuffing than we've ever seen. Not only do we have those side dishes, but it's also a family tradition to make broccoli rice casserole, green bean casserole, mashed potatoes and gravy, buttered corn, glazed carrots, and hot dinner rolls, not to mention delicious homemade pumpkin pie and other sweet dessert treats. Why do we prepare all this food and feast on it? Because Thanksgiving is a festival of abundance. The holiday aroma greets each family member as they enter the front door and welcomes them into the pumpkin-spiced celebration of overflowing goodness. We give thanks because there is plenty for everyone.

When I was growing up, my parents were responsible for decorating the church sanctuary for Thanksgiving Sunday every year. We children always looked forward to it because it was such an exciting time. On the Saturday before Thanksgiving, the whole family would go to the farmer's market. Our parents took us from stall to stall, and we would buy many large bunches of carrots and lots of fresh cucumbers, zucchinis, eggplants, tomatoes, and more. We would buy every kind of vegetable we could find—and lots of them.

After we had finished in the vegetable section, we would move on to the fruits, purchasing bushels of crunchy apples. Following this, we would go through the bread stalls and pick out the most beautiful loaves of fresh bread. Besides this, we would buy tall cornstalks, gourds, the largest pumpkins we could find, and bales of hay. Did we then go home and have a feast with this bounty? No, it was all for the display that would be set up on the steps leading to the altar at the front of the church sanctuary. It was truly a cornucopia of foods, and it symbolized the blessings of God we were celebrating.

We would spent the rest of the day at the church, setting up that beautiful display for Sunday morning. We used traditional cornucopia baskets, and we loved stuffing them so full that the food was spilling out. The church never looked so good as when there was abundance spread out across the altar. We were thankful for the harvest, and the foods that were displayed represented the abundance God had provided for His people. Abundance is a blessing, and it is part of God's shower of love for His people. God has a cornucopia of provision for you too! You are part of His plan of prosperity.

We decorated the church in this way for many years, but I remember one year in particular. I was sitting in about the middle of the sanctuary that Sunday. We almost always had visitors at the church, but especially at Thanksgiving, Christmas, and Easter. The pastor was standing before us, preaching a good Thanksgiving message, and I was looking at all that good food spread around the altar. I could only imagine what our visitors that day were thinking. But it appeared that one particular visitor had been waiting for the pastor to bless the food so we could eat because, halfway through the preaching, he got up and walked straight to the front of the church.

Everybody became very quiet, and I could sense that all eyes were on that visitor. The pastor stopped his preaching and looked directly at the man, who briefly paused. For a moment, the man seemed to be frozen. Then, just as quickly as he had stopped, he walked right up to the pile of food and started rifling through it. He seemed to be looking for something in particular. When he found a nice big crunchy apple, he grabbed it out of the display, turned around, and held up his prize for all to see. Then he took a big bite out of it and walked back to his seat and sat down.

Most of the people in the church were probably wondering what that stranger thought he was doing. I was just a little kid, and I remember thinking, "I wish we could all just get up and eat an apple! I'm hungry, and there's so much good food. Why don't we just get up and start eating it like that visitor?"

My friend, God has so much abundance available for us that we need to be like that man who confidently got up, walked toward the abundance, and took what he wanted. God's abundance is spilling out in front of us, and I want to receive what He says is mine. I want to take hold of the abundance God has given for us, His children, as we travel along the pathway of His overflowing provision. Do you want to receive this abundance? Let the Spirit give you a vision of it.

ENVISION A CHANNEL OF BLESSINGS

In various teachings, including the following, Jesus spoke about God's desire to give us abundance:

> A thief has only one thing in mind—he wants to steal, slaughter, and destroy. But I have come to give you **everything in abundance, more than you expect—life in its fullness until you overflow.** (John 10:10 TPT)

"Everything in abundance"!

"More than you expect!"!

"Life in its fullness"!

"Until you overflow"!

In the above Scripture, there is nothing at all to indicate that this full and overflowing abundance was just for Jesus. No, He directed His statement to us, saying, "I have come to give **you** everything in abundance." This promise is for you! Say it out loud:

"The abundant life is for me."

Abundance comes into our lives in many ways and in many different forms. According to the dictionary, *abundance* means "a very large quantity of something"; "the state or condition of having a copious quantity of something; plentifulness"; "plentifulness of the good things of life; prosperity."[3] That all sounds good to me. Why is it, then, that in some church circles, *prosperity* has become a dirty word? I can only assume it's because the word has been misunderstood and possibly misused. True prosperity is having enough to meet your own needs, and also enough left over to meet the needs of someone else. What could possibly be wrong with that?

The Bible has much to say about abundance and prosperity in the life of the believer. I have already mentioned 3 John 1:2, which very specifically talks about having an abundance of prosperity that comes through your spirit, your soul, and your physical body. In other words, as I have stated previously, God wants you to prosper in every way! I encourage you to write this statement down right now and say it out loud:

"God wants me to prosper in every way."

As we know, real prosperity starts in our spirits, but then it flows to our souls and ultimately manifests in our physical bodies and also in our finances and material goods.

In Psalm 35:27, the psalmist declares,

> Let them shout for joy and be glad, who favor my righteous cause; and let them say continually, "Let the LORD be magnified, who has pleasure in the prosperity of His servant." (NKJV)

This verse, also, speaks about the well-being of God's people. It is self-explanatory. God not only wants you to prosper, but He also wants you to shout His praises about it! As mentioned in chapter 1, at the end of each mystery chapter, including this one, there are

---

3. Lexico.com, Oxford University Press, © 2021.

additional decrees you can shout into the atmosphere, declaring God's truth about your abundance and thereby bringing glory to His name!

Remember that one of the foundational truths in the biblical big picture of abundance is that wealth is a gift from God. In Deuteronomy 8, Moses gave the Israelites both a caution and a promise from God in this regard:

> You say in your heart, "My power and the might of my hand have gained me this wealth." And you shall remember the LORD your God, **for it is He who gives you power to get wealth**, that He may establish His covenant which He swore to your fathers, as it is this day.   (Deuteronomy 8:17–18 NKJV)

What does God give us power to get? Wealth. If we get it, we cannot assume that our own power or the might of our hands have done it: *"It is He who gives you power to get wealth."*

Again, this scriptural promise is directly tied to obedience—a major element in learning how to manifest abundance in our lives. As believers, we must understand first that all good things, including abundance of every kind, come from God and through God, and we must determine to honor Him with the abundance He brings us.

God wants to bless you so that you can be a blessing to the world around you. Abundance is not a greedy concept. I'm not talking about stockpiling or hoarding wealth, storing it in some dirty corner where moths and rust can corrupt it. (See Matthew 6:19–21.) I'm talking about opening your life so that you can become a channel into which God can invest His blessings, and then through which He can pour them out to those who need them. If God uses you in this way, everywhere you go, there will be a flow from heaven to earth, a flow of divine abundance of prosperity that will fill not only your life, but also the lives of all those you touch. Do you want this?

GOD WANTS TO BLESS YOU SO THAT YOU CAN BE A BLESSING TO THE WORLD AROUND YOU.

REFRESH YOUR SPIRITUAL FIELD OF VISION

NUMBERS AS SUPERNATURAL SIGNS

God wants me to keep His promises of abundance in my spiritual field of vision. I believe that is why He has shown me that the numbers 818 can be a supernatural sign of His abundant blessings. God shows me this group of numbers quite often. In fact, every morning and night, I invariably look at the clock at 8:18 a.m. and again at 8:18 p.m. This happened to me over and over and over until I finally caught on. "I think You're speaking to me," I said to the Lord. "I think You cause me to look at the clock at 8:18 because You have something to teach me, and I need to listen."

What is special about these numbers in terms of God's unlimited abundance? First, they serve to remind us of Deuteronomy 8:18. We need to *remember* the Lord because He's the one who gives us power to get wealth. And every morning and every night, God reminds me of this truth.

These numbers also point us to Isaiah 8:18: *"Here am I and the children whom the* LORD *has given me!* **We are for signs and for wonders** *in Israel from the* LORD *of hosts, who dwells in Mount Zion"* (NKJV). "We are for signs and for wonders"—that word is for you and for me too.

Here is the connection between these two verses: if we allow the Lord to give us the power to get wealth, and we use that wealth to glorify His name, we become signs and wonders from God to those around us.

God reminds me of these truths not only with 8:18 on the clock but also in other ways. More than once, I have gone to a hotel to check in, and the person at the front desk has said to me, "Mr. Mills, you're in room 818." In Los Angeles County, there's an 818 area code, which is the area code of some of America's wealthiest citizens, celebrities, and movie stars. I often receive phone calls from that area code, usually from someone I don't know. I always answer in the same way:

"Hello, Joshua Mills speaking."

"Joshua?" they say questioningly.

"Yes, this is Joshua," I reply.

"Oh, I'm sorry," they say, "I've got the wrong phone number," and they hang up. I know that call from the 818 area code was a reminder to me that I am blessed to be a blessing. I'm so glad that my heavenly Father gives me power to get wealth so that I can live as a sign and a wonder before others.

I encounter the number sequence 818 so much that I know it's not about me; it's about God and His plan of flowing His abundance through me. God speaks in many different ways, and we need to pay attention to how He is speaking today.

Another number pattern that I often see is 111 or 1111—these are significant biblical numbers concerning abundance too. Maybe you've also seen them often? If you have noticed them and wondered what the Spirit was attempting to communicate to you, consider the following verses from Deuteronomy:

And may the LORD, the God of your ancestors, multiply you a thousand times more and bless you as he promised!
(Deuteronomy 1:11 NLT)

You must love the LORD your God and always obey his requirements, decrees, regulations, and commands. (Deuteronomy 11:1 NLT)

But the land you are crossing the Jordan to take possession of is a land of mountains and valleys that drinks rain from heaven.
(Deuteronomy 11:11 NIV)

These verses speak of an exponential multiplication of blessing, a reminder to follow the divine instructions in order to cross over and possess the divine promise—which, remember, is a land *flowing* with an unlimited supply of milk and honey. (See Deuteronomy 6:3.)

In addition, Psalm 111 is an amazing Bible passage about God's provision. This psalm speaks about:

- remembering the works, wonders, and power of the Lord.

- recognizing that God provides food, continually remembers His covenant, and sends redemption to His people.

All of these things sound like great abundance to me! This is abundance for spirit, soul, and body.

As you can see, God sometimes speaks to us through biblical numbers to remind us of His eternal, covenantal promises. Many times, people see numbers appearing in sets, such as 111, 222, 333, 444, and 555. When this happens to me, it always indicates spiritual alignment and progression in my walk of faith. Hebrews 11:1 says, *"Faith shows the reality of what we hope for; it is the evidence of things we cannot see"* (NLT). The Spirit is setting our lives into proper order, and we must move in synchronization with Him.

Ask the Spirit to reveal His messages to you. He may even send an angel to you to confirm the message that He is bringing.[4] For example, I've learned that when God speaks to me through the numbers 111 and 1111, it is a reminder that abundance is flowing to me so that abundance can flow through me. Let's acknowledge this fact together by making it personal and speaking it out loud:

"Abundance is flowing to me so that abundance can flow through me."

HOLD ON TO HIS PROMISES!

God has given each of us many wonderful promises. While we all share a number of the promises given in His Word—such as for salvation, the gift of the Holy Spirit, and abundance—when it comes to His individual plans for us, what He has promised me is somewhat different from what He has promised you. Some promises are very personal, while others are very public. Moreover, certain of God's promises to us seem somewhat manageable; we can see how they might easily come to pass. But other promises are so big and appear to be so impossible that we wonder how they could ever be fulfilled. Additionally, some promises seem to be at hand, while others still seem to be very far away.

---

4. I speak more about this topic in chapter 10 of my book *Encountering Your Angels* (New Kensington, PA: Whitaker House, 2020).

God knows what is needed to fulfill every promise He has bestowed on us, and when He assigns His angels to us, He gives them very specific instructions for carrying it out. God knows your need for strength, joy, and perseverance, and He has sent angels with the missing pieces to put it all together and make it all happen. Angels of abundance are at work in your life to move God's words from promises to realities. So, hold on to His promises!

FOCUS ON THREE WORDS: *REMEMBER*, *POWER*, AND *WEALTH*

Deuteronomy 8:18 contains three very specific words that I want you to focus on as you read and meditate on this verse. These words jumped out at me as I was studying this Scripture:

> And you shall **remember** the LORD your God, for it is He who gives you **power** to get **wealth**, that He may establish His covenant which He swore to your fathers, as it is this day. (Deuteronomy 8:18 NKJV)

I encourage you to take time to write down these three words, or at least to circle them in this book: *remember, power,* and *wealth.* Let's explore each of the words individually.

REMEMBER

God doesn't want you to forget Him or His promise of wealth. The fact that He tells us, through Moses, to remember shows that it is easy for us to forget. If God thought you would automatically remember Him and His purposes of abundance, keeping them in focus, He would not have taken the time to remind you to remember. This is something worth remembering!

God wants us to remember because He knows that the enemy will try to cause us to forget. As the situations of our lives change, we often shift our focus to our circumstances and lose sight of what God has said to us. Our minds easily and often forget important matters. That's why we have to make an effort to remember this essential point that God gives us power to get wealth. We must train ourselves to remember it. We must strategically place reminders around us to secure our memory of this truth. If you forget that God gives you power to get wealth, it can adversely affect your life and the lives of many others. This is why we must develop an abundance mindset.

Someone might say, "I could never forget that God wants to make me wealthy," but obviously there are reasons why God specifically told us that we need to remember Him and His promise to us. Let me offer several reasons for remembering, which are connected to our tendency to become easily distracted by our circumstances.

TO KEEP TRUSTING IN GOD

One reason God has told us to remember is because we might become so successful that we start to believe our own ability and natural talents have created our profound success, that our own human achievement has brought us to this place in our lives, that our own feet have placed us on the mountaintop, our own hands have caused us to succeed. (See Deuteronomy 8:17.) Human nature always wants to take the credit and receive the reward.

If you can see that your success is not your own doing, that's half the battle. Your flesh will want to take the credit, so God says to remember and keep things in proper perspective and in right alignment. If you remember that your success in life is the Lord's doing, it will keep you from becoming prideful, which is vital: *"Pride goes before destruction, and a haughty spirit before a fall"* (Proverbs 16:18).

God said to remember because He doesn't want you to fall. Far too many people, when they experience success and riches, have a sudden spiritual collapse. God wants you to rise higher and higher. He wants you to achieve more and more. He wants you to be ever more successful. And the only way that can happen is if you remember that it's all from Him and that He deserves all the glory. Remembering keeps your heart in an attitude of worship, and isn't that what it's all about? Yes!

Our goal is not to become successful so that others will say, "Wow, aren't they wonderful!" We want to succeed, prosper, and walk in abundance so our lives can reveal the light of Christ. Our deepest desire is that Jesus will be seen everywhere we go, that His touch will be felt wherever we minister, and that His hope will be experienced by others when we come upon situations that seem hopeless. We want the whole world to know that it is Jesus Christ, the Hope of the World, who has brought us help and, through us, brought others help as well.

TO RELY ON YOUR TRUE SOURCE

Another reason the Lord has told us to remember Him and His promise is that the enemy of our souls would love nothing more than for us to experience financial trouble by forgetting who our ultimate Source of wealth is. Nothing in the natural has brought you supernatural provision, so remember to give God the glory when you receive it. Remembering will keep your eyes toward heaven, realizing that Jesus Christ is your Source. He is Jehovah-Jireh, the Lord God your Provider. He is El Shaddai, the God of more than enough.

God doesn't put any stipulations on His promises except for our obedience. Circumstances do not change what He has said to us. As a musician, I know what a financial hit musicians have taken in recent years. They used to be able to sell an album as a CD for $20. However, they took a large cut when albums began to be available as digital downloads for about $9.99. Beyond that, individual songs could be purchased separately. Many people just wanted one song from a particular album, and they were often only charged 99 cents for it. Then, amazingly, along came online streaming services that offered all of our music, paying the musicians much less than one cent per stream. In a few short years, for musicians, much of the profit went out of the music industry.

If I had to rely on the sale of CDs to support my family and ministry, I would be in trouble. The decrease in profits in the natural has been devastating. But that's in the natural. God's promise of wealth is not for everyone *except* musicians. He loves us too! Because God has taught me to live in the realm of the Spirit, I am doing better today than I was when I was selling music CDs for $20 each. Why? Because I remember that it is not my sales ability or the personality of the people at the resource tables during my ministry trips that will make my ministry a success. The same principle applies to the sales of my books or any other items. It is not the look of a book cover that a particular graphic designer has created that will bring me provision. I remember that it is *the Lord* who gives me the power to get wealth, and it doesn't matter what circumstances I might find myself in. God desires to prosper me in every situation. And His promise is for you, as well, no matter what the circumstances of your life.

JESUS CHRIST IS YOUR SOURCE. HE IS JEHOVAH-JIREH, THE LORD GOD YOUR PROVIDER. HE IS EL SHADDAI, THE GOD OF MORE THAN ENOUGH.

We can sit and complain about how the big technology companies are "taking over" the United States and other countries, and about all the other changes that are happening in our modern society that may affect our perceived economic security, or we can lift our eyes up higher and begin to thank God that He has "technology" in the heavenlies that outweighs every resource on earth. Our pathway of provision comes directly from the glory realm into our lives, from the divine supernatural into the earthly natural.

It doesn't matter if we experience a slowdown in the world's economic systems. It doesn't matter if you face mounting debt and feel like you are in an impossible situation. It doesn't matter if you get an unexpected bill in the mail or if large expenses suddenly arise for you. It doesn't matter if you experience a job loss or a demotion. At the end of the day, whatever has happened, remember that *"it is* [the Lord your God] *who gives you power to get wealth."*

Again, it is unfortunately very easy for us to forget what God has told us and what He has done in our lives and in others' lives. Years ago, I prayed, "God, if You want me to remember certain things, then I need to know how." So many wonderful things have happened to me and, when they occurred, I thought I would never forget them—but somehow I often did. I had to get in the habit of immediately recording testimonies or writing down God's provision and answers to prayer. Far too often, this scenario happens to me: people will give me wonderful testimonies during a service, and I will think, "I need to put that in one of my books. That's so great!" But then, after I return to my hotel and call Janet, although it is only about two hours later, I can't remember some of the details. "You should have written it down," Janet will always say. And she's right!

I challenge you to write down Deuteronomy 8:18. This is your promise, and you can't afford to forget it. Writing down what we want to remember for our spiritual growth isn't an unusual concept—it is actually similar to what most of us do before we go on a shopping trip. For example, whenever I go to a huge retail store, I have to make a list beforehand of what I plan to buy. To me, these stores are like the world's largest maze. If I enter the store without a list, I will start looking at other items that stretch out before me and quickly forget what I originally came for. If Janet sends me to the store for something, she always writes it down for me so that I don't forget.

Another way to be sure you remember something is to constantly expose yourself to it. The more you expose yourself to God's promises, the less likely you will be to forget them. Writing them down works well, but it won't do you any good unless you choose to regularly review those truths.

Some people write down a promise and then shove it into their Bible or another book they are reading and soon forget it. I've done that myself, and I'm sure you have too. Recently, I was going through some books at our home. I love books, and I have lots of them. I keep about ten books beside my bed that I'm reading and studying at any one time. I have books in the kitchen and books beside the couch in the living room. And I have many books in my office. These are all books that I use and love. I'm always reading something.

As I was going through those books that day, I flipped through the pages of one particular book to remind myself of its main themes, and as I did, a little note fell out. The note contained the words to a beautiful little song our son Lincoln had composed. The Lord had put those words in his heart, and he had written them down. The note was dated, and as I read it, I wept. I had forgotten that he had even written the song. It had meant a lot to me at the time, but I had hidden the note away and forgotten about it.

My suggestion is that after you record on a piece of paper the promises of God that especially speak to you, then place the paper in a convenient place in your home or office so you can read the verses often and fill your mind with the wonder of them. You might want to write down Scriptures on several notes and place them in different places around your home.

I find that a good place to display a promise is on my mirror in the bathroom. That way, every single day, when I brush my teeth and comb my hair, I am reminded of it. Another good place is on the refrigerator. Many of us make far too many trips to the fridge every day, so it is a wonderful place to display something we want to remember. It might be helpful to schedule reminders on your smart phone several times a day so that you keep in mind God's promises of provision throughout the day. Whatever you do, keep God's promises in front of your face, and when you see them, your spirit will be exposed to them.

TO SEAL THE TRUTH IN YOUR SPIRIT

A third reason God told us to remember Him and His promises is that repetition helps us to retain information and establish truth in our lives. This is the reason believers down through the ages have made it a habit to memorize as many of the great biblical promises as they can. They not only memorize them, but they also recite them in public and in private. This is even better than just writing down the promises and even reviewing them. When you speak out a promise, it seals it in your spirit—and hell trembles. This is one of the best ways to activate your faith, and the very best way to activate angelic activity on your behalf.

Marketing experts have developed what they call the Rule of Seven. They believe that if you hear something repeated seven times or more, you will take action on it. You might not take that action if you hear it just once or twice.

The first time you speak out a promise God has given you, you will likely feel something, for God's Word is powerful, and it moves us, stirring our faith. But the second time you speak it out, you will feel much more. The more you speak it out, the more your faith will rise, and you will lay hold of the promise. Each time you speak it out, you will be encouraged. Do this every day for seven days, and I promise that something will begin to shift in your spirit. You may have believed the promise at the first, but then you will really *know* that every word of it is true.

During the week, we all hear many different voices that vie for our attention and allegiance. Aside from the Lord's voice, make sure your voice—grounded in God's Word—is the strongest of all. You must believe what you are saying—above and beyond anything others might say that is contrary to the Word. Again, this will activate angels on your behalf in response to God's command:

> Bless the LORD, you His angels, that excel in strength, that do His commandments, hearkening to the voice of His word.
>
> (Psalm 103:20)

When you speak God's Word, angels are set into motion. Therefore, when you speak the promise of Deuteronomy 8:18, angels of abundance begin to move into action, and you will see the supernatural results.

POWER

Next, let's look at the word *power*. The Hebrew word *koach*, translated as *"power"* in Deuteronomy 8:18, has several meanings. When I first looked up this word, in addition to the meanings of "strength," "power," and "might," I was surprised to see that it can refer to "a small reptile."[5] That didn't mean much to me. Then I learned that the word could denote a chameleon.[6] A chameleon has the ability to conceal itself so that it is not immediately detected, and that is its strength.

What does this have to do with God giving you the power to get wealth? Well, there may have been people who tried to get in the way when they heard you were about to be blessed. They saw you heading toward God's abundance, and they felt compelled to jump in front of you and do what they could to stop it from happening. People can be odd, and they can do all sorts of strange things, such as explaining to you why you are not qualified for such a blessing. When you get it in your spirit that God is about to bless you, and you start telling people about it, they may come up with reasons why it just can't happen, including:

---

5. The Old Testament Hebrew Lexicon—King James Version or New American Standard, which is the Brown, Driver, Briggs, Gesenius Lexicon (public domain), BibleStudyTools, https://www.biblestudytools.com/lexicons/hebrew/nas/koach.html.
6. *Strong's Exhaustive Concordance of the Bible*, STRONG, (© 1980, 1986, and assigned to World Bible Publishers, Inc. Used by permission. All rights reserved.), #3581.

- "Don't you remember what you did in the past? Other people will never let you forget it."

- "Don't you remember where you came from? Everyone else does."

- "Your family has never been all that blessed. You must be cursed."

- "What makes you think you'll do something greater than others have done?"

On and on it goes. I think you know what I'm talking about. You've probably been "messed with" a few times, and it may have held you back in the past, but that has to end. Right now, you are receiving a revelation that will take you higher. This revelation is opening a door of abundance in your life like you have never known before. God's power is coming on you, and it will put you in the right place at the right time with the right people—and no one else has to see it coming. What is coming? Some camouflaging power, just like a chameleon has. It's the ability to blend into a scene without detection and therefore avoid opposition.

If you can gain some spiritual insight to see what God is doing behind the scenes, you will begin to move in an inconspicuous way into the favor that He has appointed for your life. You are about to surprise everyone with the way God shows up and shows off through you.

I think there's a deeper reason why this power can be compared to a chameleon. Earlier, I mentioned Psalm 103:20. Let's read that verse again and let the Holy Spirit speak to our hearts:

> Bless the LORD, you His angels, that excel in strength, that do His commandments, hearkening to the voice of His word.
>
> (Psalm 103:20)

The word translated as *"strength"* here is *koach*, the same word that is translated as *"power"* in Deuteronomy 1:18. God's angels *"excel in strength."* We might translate this word "strength" as "power." If there is any doubt in your mind that you have angels with you to bring abundance into your life, that doubt can now be abolished. God said His angels excel in power. They do His commandments. They hearken to the voice of His Word. Chameleon-like, they are invisible and go undetected by the natural eye, but they are right with you, surrounding you and awaiting your Word-directed orders. God has given you the "strength" of angels, or what I call "angel power," to help you achieve divine wealth and unlimited abundance! Again, we will talk more about this in chapter 7 when we discuss Divine Mystery #6.

WEALTH

When some people think of wealth, they envision rich and famous people who live in Beverly Hills and celebrities whose pictures are on magazine covers. Other people think of the queen of England living in Buckingham Palace. Still others might even think of somebody driving down the road in a $70 million 1963 Ferrari 250 GTO automobile. (Yes, it's true. Such a car really exists!)[7]

While some of those things might be nice, in certain ways, they could also be a curse. For example, if you were a celebrity living in Beverly Hills, you might constantly be hounded by paparazzi. And if your photo were on the covers of magazines, that might open the door for people to critique you. If you were the queen, your life would continually be under a microscope, scrutinized by people around the world. And if you owned that Ferrari, can you imagine how much worry that might cause you each time you drove the car that something would happen to it—or can you picture the bill to fix the engine of a $70 million car!

The wealth that Deuteronomy 8:18 is speaking about is not just any kind of wealth, and it does not bring us distress. The Hebrew word translated as *"wealth"* is *chayil*, among whose meanings are "a force," "an army," "wealth," "virtue," "valor," and "strength."[8] This is the kind of wealth that God has given you power for—and the kind He wants you to remember. This is the kind that moves forward in your life with supernatural force. This wealth is like an army filled with valor and strength! It has the ability to eradicate every barrier of poverty, destroy every curse of the enemy, and displace all lack and insufficiency so that you will abound in every good thing! It's not just a little pile here or a little blessing there—it is a continual force of

---

7. Joel Stocksdale, "1963 Ferrari 250 GTO sells for $70 Million," *Autoblog*, June 4, 2018, https://www.autoblog.com/2018/06/04/1963-ferrari-250-gto-70-million/.
8. *Strong's*, #2428.

wealth that constantly knocks down the false idols of pain, suffering, and debt that the enemy has tried to make you bow to.

Those idols are coming down! Say goodbye to poverty. Say goodbye to lack. Say goodbye to insufficiency. You're not going to have any time to focus on those scarcities anymore—you're going to be too busy remembering the Lord, focused on what He is doing in your life and the vision He has for you. This is your promise! You need to speak it! Get the angels moving on it!

Make the heavenly vision personal by proclaiming Deuteronomy 8:18 in the following way as a prayer to the Lord:

> With profound respect, I will remember You, my Lord and my God, for You give me such powerful force—the same kind that the angels use—to supernaturally remove, like an army moving forward in battle, any indication of poverty in my life. And, through this, You are confirming Your covenant with me—a covenant of divine prosperity and an abundance of wealth!
>
> Father, I thank You for moving me into the realms of divine wealth. I ask that You would fill my life to overflowing with all of the goodness of heaven. Thank You that You love me so much. Thank You that You are releasing miracles of every type in these end times. Touch me with your miracle-working power. And Lord, for those who are sick, I ask you to prosper their health, giving them the healings they need. For those who are in family crises, prosper them with love for one another and with wisdom to work out their situations to Your glory. For those who are in physical need, open the windows of heaven and pour out blessings upon them as only You can. Lord, I thank You for doing this, in Jesus's mighty name. Amen!

Divine Mystery #1 has been uncovered and is being absorbed into your spirit and lifestyle. On to unlocking the second of *7 Divine Mysteries*—and soon you will be manifesting an overflow of abundance in every area of your life!

DECREES OF ABUNDANCE

As you decree the following truths, there will be a shift into manifesting unlimited abundance. Spirit, let it flow!

- *Heaven's provision is my daily vision.*

- *The abundance I see is the abundance I receive.*

- *My spirit is filled with the blessings of plenty.*

- *My mind is filled with overflowing abundance.*

- *My life is filled with God's abundance in every way.*

- *As I focus on Christ, everything I need is added to me.*

- *My heavenly Father is the God of abundance, and I am a child of abundance.*

CHAPTER 3

DIVINE MYSTERY #2: WHAT YOU SAY CREATES A WAY

"For by your words you shall be justified,
and by your words you shall be condemned."
—Matthew 12:37

Because I was born and raised in Canada, most people assume that I like colder temperatures. But nothing could be further from the truth! When I think about wintertime, my mind is filled with memories of walking to school with my friends through knee-deep snow. When we trudged through the snowdrifts, it caused snow to fall into our boots, and by the time we arrived at school, our socks were soaking wet. There was an area inside the classroom where we would place our wet boots, and then, as the teacher instructed, we would drape our wet socks over the radiator heaters to dry. You can imagine the "beautiful" aroma that filled our classroom all winter long...yes, unfortunately, I can smell it even now. For me, that's the overall feeling I have about winter. It reeked!

SPEAKING IN FAITH

As a child, longing for warm weather, I dreamed about the day when I would see a palm tree in real life. My grandparents often took winter vacations to warm destinations like California and Florida, sending me postcards of the San Diego Zoo and Walt Disney World. Those places seemed like paradise to me. And for that reason, I would often announce to my parents, "When I grow up, I'm going to live in Florida or California." To which my parents would quickly respond, "You can't move to Florida; there are hurricanes there. And California has too many earthquakes." I would reply, "I can't stay in Canada—we have too much snow!"

At one point, my parents got so tired of hearing me talk about living in Florida or California that my mother asked, "Isn't there anything else you can think about?" But there didn't seem to be anything else to think or talk about. I was determined not only to visit these places but also to live in them. Years later, what I had said created a way for my declarations to become reality.

At the age of nineteen, I was invited by Pastor Bill Wilson to lead worship at an extended revival he was conducting near San Diego. This was my very first invitation to minister in the United States. I agreed to lead worship for one week. At the end of that week, there was an airline strike, and I couldn't return home, so Pastor Bill asked me to lead worship for another week. At the end of that week, he asked me to be part of the ministry staff at the church where he pastored—in Spring Hill, Florida.

Since the revival Pastor Bill was conducting in San Diego was ongoing, he asked me to lead worship for him at his Florida church services on Sunday, and to join him at times for the revival in San Diego during the week. So, God answered both of my prayers in that moment. I applied for a work visa and was living in both Florida and California at the same time! Get ready for God to answer your unusual prayers, too, as you learn how to tap into His flow of unlimited abundance.

THERE IS POWER IN YOUR WORDS.

The Bible tells us that we can have whatever we speak in faith. (See, for example, Mark 11:23.) When I was a boy, I didn't understand this concept, but because I believed that one day I would live in a warmer climate, what I declared happened. Faith is a spiritual force that must be decreed. Whenever you choose to speak in faith, you direct divine activity around your life. If you don't like the way you feel physically, speak to your body and command it to change. If you need an increase of provision, command it to come. This is the second divine mystery concerning manifesting supernatural abundance—*what you say creates a way.*

As we explore principles for manifesting abundance, including speaking in faith, let's review what true abundance is. As we discussed earlier, when thinking about abundance, some people automatically assume it means to be overflowing in financial and monetary ways alone. And although that is part of abundance, it is not all that abundance represents. The Bible says,

> And **God is able to bless you abundantly,** so that **in all things at all times, having all that you need,** *you will abound in every good work.*   (2 Corinthians 9:8 NIV)

God is taking you into places you never thought you could go. He is opening new portals of glory, new doorways of access for you. His plans for you are good. They are plentiful. They are filled with abundance, with overflowing promises and miracles. Get ready, because your miracle is coming now!

HOLY SPIRIT, WE OPEN WIDE EVERY PART OF OUR BEING TO RECEIVE EVERYTHING YOU HAVE FOR US, AND WE THANK YOU FOR BREAKTHROUGH.

The Lord spoke to my wife, Janet, and me the following truth (mentioned in chapter 1 in the context of Psalm 1:3), which talks about being like a fruitful tree: "Abundance belongs to every believer in every season of life." Regardless of what it looks like in the natural, God has promised victory and breakthroughs, and they are available to you right now.

WHAT ARE YOU THINKING?

What we say creates a way, but what we speak starts in our minds and emotions. *"For out of the abundance of the heart the mouth speaks"* (Matthew 12:34). The way we think and the way we assess our circumstances makes all the difference.

RECOGNIZE YOUR TRUE ENEMIES

If you are struggling with difficulty or opposition, if you are troubled on every side, if it seems like you are constantly dealing with problems, who do you blame for these issues? Who seems to be thwarting you? If you can't identify your true adversary, you'll never overcome him. You can't take authority over an adversary you don't recognize.

Many people look at the antagonistic individuals or situations in their lives as their enemies. Other people blame a particular political party for their troubles. Still others consider a certain foreign country to be their main enemy. While opposition may come to us in the form of other people and entities working against us—and while our own lack of spiritual maturity may even be a contributing cause of our problems—the Bible is clear on who our real enemies in this life are:

> *For our struggle is not against flesh and blood [contending only with physical opponents], but against the **rulers**, against the **powers**, against the **world forces** of this [present] darkness, against the **spiritual forces of wickedness** in the heavenly (supernatural) places.*
> (Ephesians 6:12 AMP)

We must recognize that when we experience difficulties, we are not ultimately dealing with people but with *"spiritual forces of wickedness"* in the heavenly or supernatural places. This reference to heavenly places is not talking about the domain where God's throne is. There are actually three heavens. Basically, the first heaven is the atmosphere around us here on earth. The second heaven, which Ephesians 6:12 refers to, is beyond that atmosphere and is the realm where demons and angels engage in spiritual battle. The third heaven is where God abides.[9]

The enemy would love nothing more than to bring us into a place where all we can see is second-heaven warfare, constant battle. If you focus on the spiritual warfare taking place in the second heaven, you may experience physical symptoms, such as a headache, an upset stomach, tension, or overall uneasiness. If you have been feeling pressure in your spirit or even your physical body, speak against that pressure right now in the name of Jesus. I join with you to command this oppression to be broken off of you. You were not created to dwell in the second-heaven places; you were born from and for God's glory.

RECOGNIZE WHERE YOU DWELL

Where were you created to dwell? The Bible says that, spiritually speaking, you are, even now, seated *"in heavenly places in Christ Jesus"* (Ephesians 2:6). This refers to the third heaven where Christ abides. You have been seated there with Him. When you speak with the authority given to you in Jesus, what you say creates the way to peace, grace, and mercy in abundance.

So, rise up! Go higher! Go farther! Open your spiritual eyes to see *"as it is in heaven"* (Matthew 6:10). See the reality of the third heaven where God abides, where there is victory. This is a realm where miracles flow with ease. It is a place of health and wholeness, a place of unlimited abundance. Paul wrote to the church in Philippi, *"My **God shall supply all your need** according to His riches in glory by Christ Jesus"* (Philippians 4:19).

If you have read my book *Power Portals*, you know that Jesus Christ is our Door, or Gateway, into heavenly glory. Jesus is our supernatural Portal, and the only way to the Father. He gives us access into the third heaven, where the Father wants us to continually live. That is why God has already seated us there. Remember how, as a boy, I was constantly saying I wanted to live in a region that has a warm climate? Similarly, we must constantly affirm that we want to experientially live in the third heaven, where God reigns supreme in every part of our lives— and He will prepare the way for us to live there.

9. For more in-depth teaching on the three heavens, please see my book *Moving in Glory Realms* (New Kensington, PA: Whitaker House, 2018).

From the vantage point of the third heaven, as we look at the earth and earthly situations, we can easily recognize that our enemies are not people, political parties, or particular nations. Our enemies are not of this world. Instead, they are evil spiritual forces, forces of demons. Whether you know it yet or not, you are engaged in spiritual warfare. So now is *not* the time to become complacent. Now is *not* the time to sit on the sidelines and merely watch what is happening. Now is the time to pray from the third heaven and speak the victory that is ours through Christ Jesus.

WHAT ARE YOU BELIEVING?

We must be honest with ourselves, asking, "What do I believe? Do I believe the truth in Christ? Do I fully believe God's Word, the Bible? Or am I, even unknowingly, believing the lies of the enemy spirit?"

I am convinced that a number of Christians actually believe many of the enemy's lies. This is so sad and should not be. Believers need to firmly stand on the truth of God's Word. Here are two spiritual truths we must recognize: (1) the enemy operates in the realm of lies, and (2) God's Spirit of glory operates in the realm of truth. We need to reject the realm of lies and move into the realm of truth in all areas of our lives. Let's look at each of these realms more closely.

REJECTING THE REALM OF LIES

Again, Satan operates in the realm of lies, and there is no truth in him. *None.* This is what Jesus said about him:

> He was a **murderer** from the beginning, and does not stand in the truth because there is **no truth in him**. When he lies, he speaks what is natural to him, for **he is a liar and the father of lies and half-truths**.
> (John 8:44 AMP)

The enemy of our souls carries a murdering spirit, which is attached to every one of his evil assignments. Back in the beginning, in the garden of Eden, he essentially murdered the first man and woman through his lies, stealing spiritual life from them and gloating over it.

When the enemy came to tempt Adam and Eve with sin, they were dwelling in a paradise, an abundant garden with overflowing provision. There was no lack. They were living in the light of God, in divine communion and relationship with the Lord of all. But when the enemy came and sowed seeds of division, he said, in effect, "I know that God told you not to eat this fruit, but I assure you that nothing bad will happen if you do. In fact, you will become like gods. That's why God didn't want you to eat it. He was just jealous. So, go ahead—eat it." Unfortunately, Adam and Eve ate; and when they did, they tasted what death was all about. For the very first time, there was a spiritual separation between them and God. Their disobedience also brought them shame, reproach, and eventual physical death. (See Genesis 3.)

When Adam and Eve sinned, the murdering spirit was passed to humankind; and, soon enough, their son Cain murdered his own brother, Abel. (See Genesis 4:1–16.) From that sad beginning, through the annals of history until now, when the enemy has shown up, he has tried to kill whatever God desires to prosper.

OPEN YOUR HEART TO THE TRUTH

If we are to have a glorious future, we must stop believing and agreeing with the lies of the enemy. *"When he lies, he speaks what is natural to him."* Why? *"For he is a liar and the father of lies and half-truths."* If something is not the whole truth, it's a lie.

There is a lot of truth-twisting going on in our world today. This means you need to keep your ears open to hear the truth from God, who is Truth. Open your heart to learn from God's Word and Spirit what is true and what is a lie—what comes from God and what comes from the enemy spirit. If you accept the lies of the enemy, you have embraced a murdering spirit that will attempt to destroy the call of God on your life.

> ## STOP AGREEING WITH THE ENEMY SPIRIT TODAY—STOP SAYING WHAT IS CONTRARY TO GOD'S WORD.

Many of the negative things that are happening in the world today do not seem to make sense. If you look at things rationally, reasonably, with a Spirit-filled mind, you have to say, "This does not make any sense at all." It is vital that we be able to discern when a demonic spirit is at work in our lives and in the world, bringing unexpected and unexplainable trouble. The enemy spirit comes to us with lies and half-truths, which cause confusion. He attempts to hold us back by building barricades or barriers in our lives.

In whatever area the enemy is trying to meddle—whether it is your provision, your health, your relationships with your family members, or even a spiritual issue within a church or ministry—his desire is to sow confusion. And he is good at it. To counteract him, we must speak words that create a way into God's presence and deliverance. Let us take a moment now to pray for each other:

> Father God, thank You that Your Spirit of Truth rules and reigns in our lives. We come into agreement with the Lord of glory that all confusion is canceled and that the curse is broken off our lives right now. We refuse to agree with the enemy's lies any longer. Thank You, Lord, that no demonic force, principality, or evil power has a stronghold or grip on us. We choose to believe and receive from the Spirit of Truth. Thank You, Lord, that every spirit of confusion must leave right now, every spirit of chaos must flee. And I thank You, Lord, that complete clarity, insight, wisdom, and revelation will saturate our lives and the lives of our friends and family members right now. In the name of Jesus Christ and by the power of the Holy Spirit, amen!

There is a breakthrough happening for you right now! Begin speaking about Jesus and all that He is doing in the world today. He is the Lord of abundance! We can live in His abundant presence every day as we speak more and more about Him.

PROMOTE GOD'S TRUTH IN THE CHURCH

The Bible calls Satan *"the accuser of our brothers and sisters"* (Revelation 12:10 NIV). Anything and everything he says is calculated to create division within the body of Christ, and we must not fall for his tactics but rather stand against his attacks. Whenever we see that the enemy spirit is attempting to get the people of God out of alignment, away from the truth in Christ Jesus, we must expose his lies.

> But **speaking the truth in love** *[in all things—both our speech and our lives expressing **His truth**], let us grow up in all things into Him [following His example] who is the Head—Christ. From Him the whole body [the church, in all its various parts], joined and knitted firmly together by what every joint supplies, when each part is working properly,* **causes the body to grow and mature,** *building itself up in [unselfish] love.*   (Ephesians 4:15–16 AMP)

It is unfortunate that some people who call themselves believers and ministers, and who say they are doing the Lord's work, speak badly about other believers and ministers. This is not the attitude God's Word teaches us to have. It is clear from Ephesians 4:15–16 that we are not yet perfect, but there are things we are to do to bring us all closer to perfection in love. The people of God—the children of God, ministers and lay people alike, all those who follow Christ—make up the body of Christ, and the Bible says that we are to build each other up, not tear each other down.

Some Christians rip each other apart with the words they say, and that's not right. God is not pleased when we, in jealousy, try to pull down others. This is nothing but self-promotion and positioning for power, the result of a competitive spirit. We are all one family, and God has called us to strengthen one another. This is especially true with regard to young believers and those starting out in ministry. We must come alongside them with our spiritual support, encouragement, and even financial resources. When we build up the body of believers, we display the love of Christ and God's heart.

How should we respond if we have a genuine issue with another believer? Perhaps it is a doctrinal issue, something we dislike or disapprove of in their personal conduct or in the way they choose to function in ministry. Do we say something publicly to shame them and condemn them? Or do we go directly to the person and speak to them about it privately? When we are led by God to talk to someone about an issue, we are to never speak about it to others, only that individual. And whatever we do must be done in love. (See Matthew 18:15–17 for the biblical response when someone has wronged you.)

Paul wrote to the Philippians:

Some, it is true, are [actually] preaching Christ out of envy and rivalry [toward me—for no better reason than a competitive spirit or misguided ambition], but others out of goodwill and a loyal spirit [toward me]. The latter [preach Christ] out of love, because they know that I have been put here [by God on purpose] for the defense of the gospel; but the former preach Christ [insincerely] out of selfish ambition [just self-promotion], thinking that they are causing me distress in my imprisonment. What then [does it matter]? **So long as in every way, whether in pretense [for self-promotion] or in all honesty [to spread the truth], Christ is being preached; and in this I rejoice.**   (Philippians 1:15–18 AMP)*

How interesting! Some people in the church say, "I don't like the way that person is preaching," or "I don't like the way they operate in ministry." In their hearts, they simply dismiss that person and their ministry. God's heart is for all people, even those you and I may disagree with. He created them, and the promise of Jeremiah 29:11 is as much for them as it is for us. This is even true of our enemies, the people we may despise. The Lord says to us all, *"For I know the plans I have for you,…plans to prosper you and not to harm you, plans to give you hope and a future"* (Jeremiah 29:11 NIV).

The fact that some people today are preaching Christ out of envy and rivalry should not surprise us. Their competitive spirit or misguided ambition has them stuck there. It was so even in Paul's time. He said that some men were not preaching Christ for the right reasons, but he rejoiced nevertheless that the gospel was being preached. And he didn't call for the expulsion of these men from the church.

Therefore, what should we do about people in our day who are preaching the gospel out of selfish ambition, who are being guided and led by the wrong motives? Do we need to call them out publicly and shame them? No. Do we need to force them out, to put them in their place? No. Paul says:

What then [does it matter]? So long as in every way, whether in pretense [for self-promotion] or in all honesty [to spread the truth], Christ is being preached; and in this I rejoice. Yes, and I will rejoice [later as well], for I know [with confidence] that this will turn out for my deliverance and spiritual well-being, through your prayers and the [superabundant] supply of the Spirit of Jesus Christ [which uploads me]. **It is my own eager expectation and hope, that [looking toward the future] I will not disgrace myself nor be ashamed in anything, but that with courage and the utmost freedom of speech, even now as always, Christ will be magnified** *and exalted in my body, whether by life or by death.*

(Philippians 1:18–20 AMP)

If Christ is being preached, who are we to say that God can't use that person? That's His business. I'm not saying that we have to come alongside, endorse, or promote those we disagree with. I'm saying that we need to take these issues to the Lord and let Him deal with them in His own way. This posture changes our outlook. Instead of agreeing with the accuser, we are agreeing with the Word of God. This perspective also allows us to live in abundant peace as we realize that we are only responsible for our own spiritual journey. We need to stay in our own lane.

The Bible says that a kingdom divided against itself cannot stand. If we are constantly attacking and criticizing each other, it won't be long before everything we have is stripped away. Strife leads to lack, but divine unity leads to abundance. Jesus reminded us that the peacemakers are the ones who are blessed. (See Matthew 5:9.) Let's speak words that open the realms of abundance, instead of words that close doors of blessing. The Lord will honor us as we honor His body.

LISTEN TO SOUND COUNSEL

I had a dream recently in which the Lord gave me this Scripture: *"Without counsel, plans go awry, but in the multitude of counselors they are established"* (Proverbs 15:22 NKJV). Personally, I love to position myself to receive wisdom from many counselors, and I want to always remain teachable. Momma Billie Deck is one of my mentors. She once told me, "You are one of the most teachable sons I have." I don't say that to brag. I say it to show that I don't know it all. I will be the first to admit it. I don't have everything perfectly together. Janet and I are simply living our lives in the grace and glory of God and with humility, saying, "Spirit of God, teach me! Correct me! Direct me! Guide me! I want to be led by You." And this should be the posture of every believer. It will keep our hearts aligned with His will so that what we speak will also be His will—and what we say will make a way for us.

Communication with God through prayer is so important in this process. Sometimes, when we look at other people or ministries, we think we see an issue that needs to be dealt with. But when we pray about it, the Lord shows us that there is actually an issue in our own hearts, not someone else's. When this happens, we must allow the Holy Spirit to minister to us, bringing His loving correction.

KNOW THE TRUTH ABOUT YOUR ANOINTING

When we think about our roles in the body of Christ, we must also consider whether we are following the truth when it comes to exercising our spiritual gifts, and not allow the enemy to discourage us in their use.

What is your anointing? Hospitality? Kingdom financing? Healing? There are many different kinds of ministry assignments and many different anointings, including prophecy, parenting, and intercessory prayer. These are all callings from God. Remember that your teachers didn't give you an anointing—anointing comes from the Lord.

When the enemy tries to attack your life, always remember that he is the accuser. His goal is to undermine you in the area of your greatest anointing by trying to make you feel shame. For instance, how does the enemy attack a powerful intercessor? He will say, "You don't know how to pray. And why would God hear *your* prayer anyway? Your prayers are pitiful. You're not even good enough to pray." Just as what you say creates the way to fruitful abundance, what the enemy says can create the way to the destruction of your gift—if you believe and act on his lies. He says what he knows will hurt you, hoping it will discourage you from exercising God's anointing. If you are an intercessor who is being attacked in this way, what should you do? *Say* your prayers! God knows your heart; the enemy doesn't. Keep praying. Keep speaking God's truth with your mouth, and the Spirit will continue to guide you along your way.

When Janet was a teenager, her mother was diagnosed with cancer. This was a very difficult time for her family as her mother suffered tremendous pain and was in and out of the hospital on quite a few occasions. One time, when Janet was at her mother's bedside, she was told by a "family friend" to leave the room immediately because she was a hindrance to her mother's miracle. This person accused her of "not having enough faith" to believe for her own mother's healing. Those words cut Janet very deeply and were extremely painful for her to hear. Today, Janet recognizes that those accusations were nothing more than the voice of the *"accuser of* [the] *brethren"* (Revelation 12:10). For if there's one area where Janet is extremely anointed, it is in the area of faith. Janet has the greatest faith of anyone I know! Often, I will call upon her specifically because of her gift of faith. Consequently, the enemy attempted to bring his evil ridicule and lies against Janet in this area. Maybe you have experienced a similar situation in your own life. Where has the enemy been attacking you the most? That is likely the place of your greatest anointing. Recognize it, and use that anointing to put the enemy to shame. Rise up and stand firm in your anointing.

Here are some other examples of how the enemy attacks believers in the area of their spiritual gifts. The gift of hospitality is a generous anointing that encourages the body of Christ and moves people to serve others. Therefore, of course, the enemy attacks people who have this gift, perhaps causing them to feel isolated from other people and less inclined to reach out to them. When people have an anointing for marriage ministry, the enemy tries to incite problems in their own marriages. For those who carry a healing anointing, the enemy attacks their physical bodies. When people carry an anointing for prosperity and provision, the enemy goes directly after their finances. Why does he do all this? Because he wants to bring shame to our most anointed places, the special places where God has called us. So, *do not believe the lies of the enemy*, and *do not shrink back*. (See Hebrews 10:38–39.) Instead, speak God's infallible truth. Say to the accuser that he is a liar, and then move forward in your calling and don't look back, knowing your secure position in the Spirit.

KEEP SPEAKING GOD'S TRUTH, AND THE SPIRIT WILL CONTINUE TO GUIDE YOU ALONG YOUR WAY.

KNOW THE TRUTH ABOUT YOUR TESTIMONY

The enemy will sometimes attack our testimony through false accusations. When Jesus ministered on earth, the Pharisees falsely accused Him, saying, *"You bear witness of Yourself; Your witness is not true"* (John 8:13 NKJV). What was going on there? Let's set the stage. Jesus was sitting, teaching in the temple in Jerusalem, and the scribes and Pharisees came in, bringing a woman caught in the act of adultery. They sat her down and began to mock her in front of Him, suggesting that she must be stoned. At first, Jesus seemed to not even hear them. When they insisted, He said, with great wisdom, *"He who is without sin among you, let him throw a stone at her first"* (John 8:7 NKJV).

Suddenly, everyone was silent. No one dared to pick up a stone. Then, one by one, the accusers began to slink away. They all knew they had sin in their lives. They had all committed wrongs, and their motives had not always been pure. No one was worthy of judging the woman. Jesus turned to her and said, *"Neither do I condemn you; go and sin no more"* (John 8:11 NKJV).

Later, Jesus continued His teaching, saying, *"I am the light of the world. He who follows Me shall not walk in darkness, but have the light of life"* (John 8:12). The Pharisees spoke up because they had an issue with Him. He had been making a fool of their self-centered religion, and a religious spirit despises whatever it cannot control. The moment it can no longer manipulate the situation, it erupts in anger. The religious spirit is the nastiest of demons.

In their anger, the Pharisees accused Jesus of not being genuine, of not having the authority to state what He was saying. He was, they said, testifying on His own behalf and had no authority to speak for God. They claimed that His testimony was not valid but worthless. That's the kind of word the enemy speaks—the word of a liar and an accuser.

Now, let me ask you: Are you being falsely accused? Has the enemy been trying to say similar things to you? Has he tried to tell you that your testimony about what God has done in your life or about what God says in His Word is invalid, worthless, or insignificant? If so, it should be no surprise because the enemy spirit never changes his ways. He will try to use the same wiles on you that he used on Adam and Eve. Why? Because he knows that Christ lives in you, and so he must try to break your spirit and bring you down. He must try to discourage you and move you out of your anointing.

God, on the other hand, is calling you to line up and move into His greater purposes for your life, the glory He has prepared for you. You must break through every barrier the enemy has erected against you and gain your freedom in Christ. God's Word declares, *"And you shall know the truth, and the truth shall make you free"* (John 8:32 NKJV). Your freedom is coming. Read God's truth; meditate on His truth; hold His truth in your heart; and then speak and act on His truth. God's truth will bring you freedom from the enemy's lies.

I love how Jesus answered the challenge of the Pharisees, and we can learn so much from what He said. This is the best way to answer the enemy when he shows up and says things like, "Your testimony is worthless. You don't matter. Your ministry is insufficient. You can't pray the right way. Nobody likes the way you teach." When the enemy lies to us, we must respond as confidently as Jesus did to the Pharisees:

> *Jesus answered and said to them,* **"Even if I bear witness of Myself, My witness is true, for I know where I came from and where I am going***; but you do not know where I come from and where I am going."* (John 8:14 NKJV)

Anyone who has been accusing you through the enemy spirit has no idea where you've been and no clue where you're going. But the One living inside you is *greater* than anything external, and He knows the plans He has for you. (See 1 John 4:4.) The Spirit of God inside you is even now breaking out and breaking through and creating a way of escape for you. Yes, enemy barriers are coming down!

God is the only One who really knows you. Even more important, He's the only One who holds your future in His hands, with an assurance of divine and overflowing abundance as you walk humbly before Him. The key is to continue to walk in the Spirit. No matter how many lies the enemy of your soul speaks against you, don't abandon God's truth for lies. Jesus says He came to give you abundant life—but the enemy comes only to steal, kill, and destroy. (See John 10:10.)

With God, we have a future. With Him, we have hope. With Him, all things are possible. If we stay strong in the Lord, the enemy cannot steal our joy, kill our callings, or destroy our divine assignments. He will not gain the upper hand in our lives or in the lives of our family members. He will not destroy our ministries. You and I will prosper in everything God has called us to do in service to Him and for His glory!

LIVING IN THE REALM OF TRUTH

As we move out of the realm of lies, we move into the realm of truth. The Spirit of glory is the realm of truth. We know that God's Spirit cannot lie. John wrote,

> But when He, the **Spirit of Truth**, comes, He will guide you into all the truth [full and complete truth]. For **He will not speak on His own initiative**, but **He will speak whatever He hears [from the Father—the message regarding the Son], and He will disclose to you what is to come** [in the future].   (John 16:13 AMP)

God's truth, which is the greatest spiritual warfare weapon you have at your disposal, brings you victory in every battle. Spiritual warfare is not about trying to fight the enemy with a physical sword. It is about avoiding his every lie, refusing to listen to his voice. It's about allowing yourself to engage completely with the Spirit of Truth, saying, "God, You are all I need. You are more than enough. You have me covered. And because of that, I know my spiritual position. I am seated with Christ in heavenly places. I am living in the abundance of every good thing."

Our focus must be on truth. When you focus on truth, then truth becomes all you speak about because it draws all your attention. God's Word is truth; we must focus on what He tells us as we read the Bible.

PROCLAIM THE TRUTH THROUGH PRAISE

When God brought the Israelites into the promised land, He gave Joshua divine instructions about what to do and how to do it:

> **Then the LORD said** to Joshua, "See, I have delivered Jericho into your hands, along with its king and its fighting men. March around

the city once with all the armed men. Do this for six days. Have seven priests carry trumpets of rams' horns in front of the ark. On the seventh day, march around the city seven times, with the priests blowing the trumpets. When you hear them sound a long blast on the trumpets, **have the whole army give a loud shout; then the wall of the city will collapse** *and the army will go up, everyone straight in."* (Joshua 6:2–6 NIV)

Joshua listened to and obeyed God's instructions. Some people may have called Joshua crazy and others may not have believed his words. There will always be those who cannot go with the flow of what God is doing. This is why certain people who have walked with you in a past season will not be able to enter with you into your future season. Why? Because they are unprepared; they are not in the place you are in their relationship with God.

Whatever you do, don't chase after people who have walked away from you. In His grace and mercy, God may have allowed them to leave because they were pulling at you and trying to hold you to something that was only for a former time in your life. God says, "I have called you to something new, something glorious, and I am leading you to where you're going." As you follow the direction of the Holy Spirit, He will bring you into new territory, creating a path to a life overflowing with abundance.

God wants to introduce you to His greater purposes and put within you a greater praise to proclaim, a greater shout to release into the atmosphere, a greater testimony to declare so you can break down all enemy barriers.

On the day when the rams' horns blasted in Jericho, the sound of the trumpets broke through the spiritual atmosphere and brought a release. The people also cried out with a great shout like a battle cry. Because of their obedience to release what God had given them to release, because of the sound of their praise, something amazing happened. The walls came tumbling down, and the people crossed over into the city.

One moment the walls of Jericho were indestructible, and the next minute God's people were climbing over what was left of those walls and entering the territory God had promised them, taking the city by storm. In the natural, it looked like an impossible feat, but God makes all things possible.

It is absolutely amazing what our obedient praises can do. They are so powerful. Even today, as you focus on God's Word and speak His promises into the atmosphere, angels are being activated to fulfill those words. What we say creates a way!

AS YOU PRAISE GOD, WALLS FALL!

You may be dealing with situations in your life that look like obstacles to the blessings you have been promised. It might seem as if the enemy has erected immovable barriers around your miracle. You may see what look like impossible walls around your family members, hemming them in to their physical or financial needs. But remember that God gave Joshua authority to release a shout and a sound that brought down every barrier—and He gives you this same authority through the power of His Holy Spirit, who is resident within you.

As a believer in Jesus Christ, when you praise God, your atmosphere changes. When you praise God, walls fall! It really is true that what you say creates a way. This should make you shout all the more.

Hallelujah, walls of poverty are coming down!

Hallelujah, enemy assignments against your abundance are being broken!

Hallelujah, barricades around your blessings are falling!

Hallelujah!

As you continue to praise God, you will access everything He has promised you, which is all contained in the finished work of Christ on the cross of Calvary. When Jesus said, *"It is finished"* (John 19:20), He meant it. It was and is finished.

The barriers of the enemy are coming down in your life. You are being loosed and released from the distractions that have tried to hold you back. The Lord is calling you into new territories of possession and new places of promise, and with them will come new abundance. The Lord is taking you up and over and beyond.

DECREE WHAT YOU NEED

The Lord told Joshua that he could take the city of Jericho, and he believed the Lord. Many believers have been struggling to take ground for their families. Do not be discouraged. Be lifted up. If God could give Joshua a city, how much more can He give you and your family? He can give you the ministry He's promised to you. He can give you the job, the relationships, the courage, and the community He's been speaking to you about.

The questions you must now ask and answer are:

- Do I understand who my real enemies are?
- Do I understand who and what to believe?
- Do I understand how to position my faith?

The way we position our faith determines our focus, and our focus must draw all our attention upon Jesus.

Since *what you say creates a way*, you must also think about and answer these questions:

- What am I speaking?
- What am I decreeing?
- What am I declaring?
- What sounds am I releasing?

Job 22:28 says, *"You will also decide and decree a thing, and it will be established for you; and the light [of God's favor] will shine upon your ways"* (AMP). When we make decrees over matters, we can see God move on them immediately. In the glory realm, things happen instantly. There is no distance of time or space. There are no hindrances to be removed. In the eternal, there are no barriers. We are not waiting for God to do something. Rather, He has given us permission to access all of His blessings. Everything has already been accomplished, and our overflowing abundance is secured.

I urge you to write down this declaration and really believe it: "My overflowing abundance is secured." You have to know it, and then you have to *say* it. Decree it right now:

"My overflowing abundance is secured."

You may need an abundance of miracles in your body for physical healing. You may need an abundance of finances for supernatural provision. You may need an abundance of eternal life for your children or your grandchildren so that they enter into salvation. You may need an abundance of love in your marriage to bring healing after conflict. Whatever you need, decree it right now by the Spirit of God. Say, "My overflowing abundance is secured through Christ in the power of the Spirit. This abundance is for my spirit, soul, and body." Come into agreement with what God is saying and doing, and your overflowing abundance will be established. This is the realm of superabundant glory that is surrounding you right now.

In this realm, we recognize that God's provisions are already available to us, as explained by Paul in Philippians 4:19. What does God supply? *All* our needs. How does He do it? *"According to His riches in glory by Christ Jesus."* He takes care of our needs through the finished work of Christ. When we see what God has done, and we recognize it fully, instead of waiting for something to happen, we become the ones who make things happen, and we do this through the Spirit.

We speak it, and then we move into it. By faith, we declare it, and then we see its manifestation. Doors, or power portals, open to us—and we choose to enter. The same Spirit who raised Christ from the dead is working in us to resurrect what was dead, lost, or looked like it was over. The Spirit of God is working in us to bring forth resurrection glory!

WHEN YOU BELIEVE WHAT YOU SAY, YOU WILL MOVE INTO IT BY FAITH.

When we fully understand the implications of the finished work of Christ in our lives, we speak the truth and then step out in faith, causing heavenly realities to manifest on earth. What we believe, we say, which creates a way. As we do this, we become movers and shakers in this world, even as God is moving and shaking things in heaven. That's the key—to see what's happening in heaven and then do it on earth.

SPEAK A "NOW" MANIFESTATION

When we make such decrees, we're not speaking on our own accord. We're not speaking from our own imaginations. We're speaking by the very Spirit of God, the Spirit of abundance, and what we speak as revelation on earth suddenly happens. God's light shines through. As we proclaim His truth, the pronouncements of our voices bring light upon our paths, and we can see our way.

When you know how to navigate according to God's truth, you will no longer be misguided or wander away from the path. *"Your word is a lamp to guide my feet and a light for my path"* (Psalm 119:105 NLT). Suddenly, you will be directed by the Holy Spirit. When this happens, the thing the enemy said you could not do, you will do. The very thing he said was no longer available to you will open to you. Why? Because God is shining His light upon you. As He gives you the words to speak, His light is ready to shine.

The Spirit of God may prompt you to speak a prophetic utterance. What is revelation in the heavens becomes prophetic on earth. It's already known in the heavenly realm, but when you receive it in your spirit and speak it out, it becomes revelation that brings provision to yourself and others. Other people didn't realize it could happen, and they didn't see it coming. But God gave you the faith to speak it; and, as you spoke it, it brought forth an anointing in the atmosphere that ushered in the abundant glory of God.

We serve a "now" God. When we trust the Spirit and are obedient to speak His "now" word, it activates a "now" manifestation. We see this process in the life of the prophet Ezekiel, who said,

*So **I prophesied as I was commanded**; and as I prophesied, there was a [thundering] noise, **and behold, a rattling; and the bones came together**, bone to its bone.* (Ezekiel 37:7 AMP)

Ezekiel obeyed the Lord by speaking what he was instructed to say, and his obedience produced a moving and shaking in the glory. (For the exciting full vision of the valley of dry bones, please read Ezekiel 37:1–14). This is how we break through the enemy's barriers—by staying in the glory, remaining steadfast, focused, concentrated, with our eyes fixed on Jesus. We are not focused on anything except the purposes of God and the overflowing truth He has spoken.

When the sound of Ezekiel's voice went forth, the manifestation of the promise began to happen. By the time Ezekiel had finished prophesying, the miracle was already manifesting. You may have looked at your situation and said, "Well, maybe I'll have what I need in two years, maybe in ten years, maybe never." Do not limit God. Again, we serve a "now" God, and as you speak and decree in the glory, spiritual realities will move from heaven to earth.

Just as God gave Joshua directions for the people to shout, may He give you a shout too. May He give you a song. May He give you His words. When Joshua and the Israelites obeyed God's directions, those Jericho walls came tumbling down. That was the promise of God coming from the heavenly realm into the earthly realm.

The sound that caused the walls of Jericho to come down is within you. It's your gift from God. Your simple words can become the greatest weapon God has given you against the assignments of the enemy. You're *not* looking at your current circumstances. You're *not* focused on what's happening around you. You *are* looking to Jesus Christ, the Author, the Finisher, the One who began it all, and the One who promises to be with you to the end of it, the One who has guaranteed your success. If you continue following Him, obeying Him, and declaring His goodness, abundance will surely manifest, for what you say creates a way.

Divine Mysteries #1 and #2 have been uncovered, and both are being absorbed into your spirit and lifestyle on your way to manifesting unlimited abundance in every area of your life. On to Divine Mystery #3 and the joy it will bring to your spiritual perspective!

DECREES OF ABUNDANCE

As you decree the following truths, you can expect to begin manifesting overflowing abundance—so much more than "just enough." Spirit, let it flow!

- *From the abundance of my heart flows the abundance of God's blessings.*

- *Every word I speak is anointed to create my future reality.*

- *I will guard my lips and only allow God's truth to flow from my mouth.*

- *As I speak God's Word, God's Word speaks back to me.*

- *I live in the truth, I speak the truth, and I walk into the truth.*

- *I am seated in heavenly places with Christ Jesus and abundance flows through me.*

- *I am anointed to carry God's abundant overflow everywhere I go.*

CHAPTER 4

DIVINE MYSTERY #3:
THE WORD YOU WORK
WILL WORK FOR YOU

"All Scripture is God-breathed [given by divine inspiration] and is profitable for instruction, for conviction [of sin], for correction [of error and restoration to obedience], for training in righteousness [learning to live in conformity to God's will, both publicly and privately—behaving honorably with personal integrity and moral courage]; so that the man of God may be complete and proficient, outfitted and thoroughly equipped for every good work."
—2 Timothy 3:16–17 (AMP)

I love the glory of God's Word. In and through this glory, I am continually changed. A few years ago, I wrote a devotional book entitled *The Glory: Scriptures and Prayers to Manifest God's Presence in Your Life.* In that book, I included seventy-seven Scriptures pertaining to the glory, with corresponding prayers and decrees. Since the book's publication, I have received so many beautiful testimonies from people who have been deeply touched and profoundly changed as they've taken time each day to read and reflect upon the power of God's Word.

I've discovered that as I immerse myself in the glory of the Word, I see things I've never seen before, and I experience things I've never experienced before. The Word of God opens supernatural possibilities for us. And the realm of God's glory is the realm of His light; so, when we read the Scriptures, we should expect a new doorway with heavenly illumination to open before us. And when it does, we're given the appointed invitation to step in and receive all that it contains.

God's Word is not only a light to our pathways, but it is also water to our thirsty souls. One day, while ministering at Calvary Campground in Ashland, Virginia, I was having lunch with Pastor Jane Lowder. As usual, she shared a beautiful testimony with me—and this time, it was about one of her tomato plants in her large garden! A few days earlier, she had noticed it was dying; moreover, it had never produced any fruit. Sister Jane had watered and fertilized and otherwise cared for the plant—she knows her plants, having been raised on a farm—but it was still unfruitful and dying.

Maybe you're feeling like that little plant right now. Don't worry, there is hope! This is only the beginning of the story. Regardless of where you are in your life right now, if you choose to "work" God's Word, I can boldly tell you that God's truth *will* work for you!

Standing in front of that little, dying tomato plant, Sister Jane listened to the voice of the Spirit, who reminded her of God's Word—this is key! Right there, in her garden, she received words of life from the Lord to speak to the plant. She peacefully declared those words and commanded life to return to it. Then she sang over the plant.

As we had lunch that day, Sister Jane told me that she had since counted eighteen little tomatoes hanging on that plant. "I want to see this miracle and take a picture of you with it," I said. I love to see the miracles of God. No miracle is too small for Him! When we finished eating, we went together to her house. Sure enough, there was the healthy-looking plant with eighteen tomatoes hanging on it. It was amazing to see and know what God had done for that formerly dead-looking, hopeless, and desolate plant. God can do the same thing for you as you choose to work His Word. This is one of the supernatural secrets to manifesting unlimited abundance.

"It's now the hottest part of the day, and the leaves are hanging down a little. They don't look their best. Would you be able to stick around for five minutes? I want to show you something," Sister Jane said to me. I told her I could, now curious about what she had in mind.

She took out a water hose and turned it on. At first, the water was hot, so she sprayed it out on the ground until she thought the temperature was just right. Then she sprayed a gentle stream of water on the soil around the bottom of the plant. Over the next few minutes, a transformation took place. In front of my eyes, the leaves of that plant perked up, becoming more vibrant and visibly stronger. Wilting leaves were now upright and perfect in appearance. "That's amazing!" I said. I hadn't had much experience in caring for plants to know they could recover so quickly when provided with water, which is such a life-giving element.

"You know, God's Word is like water," Sister Jane said. How right she is! When we receive Jesus, the Word of God (see John 1:1,14), we receive *"rivers of living water"* (John 7:38) that we need to make us spiritually strong and provide us with supernatural refreshment, even in the most intense heat of our daily lives. Jesus tells us, *"Whoever believes in me, as Scripture has said, rivers of living water will flow from within them"* (John 7:38 NIV; see also John 4:10). Please understand this: the revelation of God's Word will cause you to rise above all your troubles, including lack and insufficiency. This supernatural revelation supersedes our natural circumstances because it is prophetic, flowing as a river from the realms of glory.

GOD'S WORD LIGHTS YOUR PATH AND WATERS YOUR SOUL.

WORKING WITH GOD'S WORD

Yes, God's Word enables us to overcome any natural difficulties. His Word triumphs over any troubles. His Word overcomes stress, anxieties, worries, depression, and self-loathing. His Word floods sickness and disease with healing waters. His Word overcomes poverty with the flow of heavenly abundance.

When I was sixteen years old, God's revelation began flowing into my life in a new way when I had a dramatic encounter with the Holy Spirit. I was born and raised in the Pentecostal environment and am a fifth-generation Spirit-filled believer. I grew up in the church, and I praise God that my parents had received salvation and were instructing me in the faith. Yet each individual has to receive a personal revelation of salvation. No one can live from someone else's revelation. Similarly, God doesn't expect you to minister or operate under somebody else's anointing; He desires to anoint *you*. He wants to give you the revelation you need for the life you will live.

Very soon after my initial encounter with the Holy Spirit began, I received a revelation about divine prosperity. This revelation has continued to grow within me from that time until now. The Spirit showed me that God desired for me to be blessed no matter what the natural circumstances looked like, no matter how large or small my paycheck was, no matter what my background was, and no matter what had happened to me in the past. God had determined that blessing would be my portion, and if I would simply believe His Word and begin to *work with His Word*, it would surely happen. He desires the same for you.

Here is a supernatural secret that I want you to write down and remember: *revelation always demands activation to produce a manifestation.*

God is looking for those who will simply *believe* His Word, *accept* the revelation of it, and *respond* to it—not just be hearers of the Word. We are to be *doers* of the Word, and in *doing the Word*—participating, working, and fully engaging with it—we will produce the fruit of the Word. (See James 1:22.) It's a miracle!

REVELATION ALWAYS DEMANDS ACTIVATION TO PRODUCE A MANIFESTATION.

Throughout the Scriptures, we see God giving His children supernatural instructions for living in abundance. Whether spiritual abundance, physical abundance, or financial abundance, when God's people responded properly to His instructions (working the Word), they received the promised miracle results. For example, Noah received supernatural instructions to build an ark and prepare for a coming flood. The Bible says, *"Noah did everything exactly as God had commanded him"* (Genesis 6:22 NLT). When he worked with God's commands, the result was his family's protection through the deluge and the Lord's blessing to live in abundance:

> *Bring forth with you every living thing that is with you, of all flesh, both of fowl, and of cattle, and of every creeping thing that creeps upon the earth; that they may breed abundantly in the earth, and be fruitful, and multiply upon the earth.* (Genesis 8:17)

Each and every day, God is giving us miracle instructions, and if we *will* obediently respond to them, they *will* produce miraculous results.

Sometimes people resist the Word of God, which causes both spiritual and natural blockage to abundance flowing into their lives. There are many reasons why people resist God's divine instructions. One of the most common reasons is personal pride. When we walk before the Lord, we must walk softly and humbly. God's ideas concerning a situation are always better than our own personal ideas. We must lay down our own agendas and plans if we are determined to enter into the life of abundance that Jesus has promised.

In the Old Testament, we find an interesting example of personal pride in the story of Naaman, an army commander who was highly regarded as a valiant soldier but suffered from leprosy. Through a series of events, he found himself standing before the door of the prophet Elisha's house with all of his horses, his chariots, his men, and his wealth. There Naaman was given this supernatural instruction from the prophet, by way of a messenger: *"Go and wash in Jordan seven times, and your flesh shall come again to you, and you shall be clean"* (2 Kings 5:10). You would assume this message would bring great joy to Naaman because the Lord had provided a supernatural solution to his problem, but that wasn't the case. Instead, Naaman became furiously angry, for several reasons:

- He had brought the equivalent of over $4 million in gold and silver[10] to pay for his doctor's bill! (See 2 Kings 5:5.)

- He was a great man and felt that he deserved a personal appearance from the prophet. He thought it would have been a tremendous honor for Elisha to come out to him and pray for this disease to be taken away. (See 2 Kings 5:9–11.)

- He wanted Elisha to magically wave his hand over him to instantly work the miracle. (See 2 Kings 5:11.)

- He couldn't understand why the prophet would tell him to go and wash in a dirty river. Naaman knew that there were cleaner waters in the Abana and Pharpar, rivers of Damascus. (See 2 Kings 5:12.)

What Elisha told Naaman didn't make any sense to his natural mind. But the Bible tells us that *"the mind of the flesh [with its sinful pursuits] is actively hostile to God. It does not submit itself to God's law, since it cannot"* (Romans 8:7 AMP). If we're going to learn how to work the Word and be empowered by the supernatural instructions of God, we have to submit our minds to the Lord and be governed by His Spirit. He will give us an abundance mindset if we allow him to.

We can actually learn a powerful prophetic message through this story. The name *Jordan* means "descender,"[11] and we know that much later on, the Jordan River became a place most famous for its spiritual water baptisms. Through the prophet, the Spirit gave an instruction for Naaman to "descend," or be fully immersed, within these waters *seven* times—God's perfect number, representing God's perfect way—so that he could transition from his old way of living into a new way of living.

Initially, Naaman wanted to do things in his own way, but he had to submit to the instruction of God if he wanted to see a change with true and lasting results. Thankfully, Naaman had other people around him who encouraged him to follow the divine instructions. When he did, he received the promised miracle.

---

10. This calculation is based on information from the footnotes in the passage from the *New International Version*, https://www.biblegateway.com/passage/?search=2%20Kings%20 5&version=NIV, and from https://www.calculateme.com/precious-metals/gold/weight/1-pounds.
11. *Strong's*, #H3383.

So he went down and plunged himself into the Jordan seven times, just as the man of God had said; and his flesh was restored like that of a little child and he was clean.   (2 Kings 5:14 AMP)

This account also highlights another supernatural secret—*you must surround yourself with people who will encourage you and motivate you toward following God's instructions and working the Word.*

Janet and I host *Glory Bible Study* online every Tuesday evening. It has become a wonderful gathering of brothers and sisters in Christ—from many denominational and cultural backgrounds—who, through divine connection, join together from all around the world. It is common to see people from Australia, South Africa, Japan, Philippines, Hong Kong, and many countries across Europe connecting with us in North America during these livestreams. There is a group of intercessors in Scotland who stay awake way into the middle of the night to join us at one o'clock in the morning their time. When we meet together in this way, we can encourage one another in the things of the Spirit.

Many of the participants have written to tell us that the Glory Bible studies have become a life-source for them because they aren't receiving these teachings in their own communities. You see, not every Christian actually believes in the supernatural power of God—but we do! We believe that God heals people today. We believe He is still working miracles today. We believe He still speaks to people today through prophetic utterances. Not only do we believe these things, but we also *know* them to be true because we see them happening on a daily basis!

One Baptist couple in their early eighties sent us a letter saying, "Everyone from young to old is a part of these weekly online meetings…and we find that there is so much refreshment that comes to us corporately as we encourage each other to work God's Word and live in the Spirit."

It's important to be surrounded not only by other believers, but, as Peter said, by those who have *"the same precious faith we have"* (see 2 Peter 1:1 NLT). Peter went on to say, *"Grace and peace be yours in abundance through the knowledge of God and of Jesus our Lord"* (2 Peter 1:2 NIV). This is a further supernatural secret to manifesting unlimited abundance: *abundance comes to us when we choose to position our lives in the knowledge of God.*

I am not saying that this process is always easy. Many times, when we are entering into something new, we go through a season of testing. Prophetically speaking, this is where the gold is put in the fire, and we find our motives being purified and our lives being refined. Sometimes it may even seem like every situation in our lives is challenging us, saying, "Do you *really* believe that the Word of God is true?" If this is the case with you, it will require a greater determination on your part to stand strong in resistance against the winds of life blowing against you.

Always remember, if God has spoken it, you can trust His Word to come to pass in your life. When you stay faithful, your season of testing leads into a new place of grace.

ABUNDANCE COMES TO US WHEN WE CHOOSE TO POSITION OUR LIVES IN THE KNOWLEDGE OF GOD.

Too many people rely on their own abilities, their employers, or others around them to meet their natural needs and desires. And yes, I think it's important to function in the abilities that God has given to you, and to work diligently and recognize the blessing that others are in your life. These are all scriptural principles. But the absolute truth that you must receive in your spirit is that God is your Provider. It's not just what He does—it's His name. Remember, He is Jehovah-Jireh, which means "the Lord will provide."

STAY IN THE SPIRIT

During our ministry travels around the world, there have been many times when people have treated us like gold. We have been extremely favored to enjoy the warm hospitality of so many wonderful people in more than seventy-five nations. The Lord has blessed us with divine connections, kingdom alignments, and the kindnesses of many people. Yet there have also been a few times when we were not treated very well at all. In those times, however, God did not forsake us. He never left us. We were still blessed, even when people attempted to do us wrong, because we learned how to stay in the Spirit by working the Word. For example:

- When an overseas ministry stole thousands of dollars from us, we chose to forgive them of the debt because that's what the Bible tells us to do. (See, for example, Luke 6:37.) When we moved in forgiveness, it opened a spiritual floodgate for thousands of dollars to be released to us in a supernatural way. To top it off, those finances came to us from the same country (although from a different source) where we had lost the other money.

- One ministry felt that it was their mission to "humble us" because they felt that our popularity had grown too large, too quickly. They made it a point to provide us with poor accommodations and very little food so we would "know what it should feel like" to be ministers of the gospel. Again, we forgave them for their unusual behavior and asked the Lord to bless them. (See Matthew 5:44.) When we did this, we received supernatural favor with the airlines and hotels—we were given complimentary first-class upgrades and courtesy stays at a five-star hotel. Because we chose to do what the Word says to do, God turned things around in our favor.

We can join with the apostle Paul in saying, *"I know what it is to be in need, and I know what it is to have plenty. I have learned the secret of being content in any and every situation, whether well fed or hungry, whether living in plenty or in want"* (Philippians 4:12 NIV). But the supernatural secret is this: "I can do all this through [Christ] *who gives me strength"* (verse 13 NKJV).

We chose to live in the breakthrough, not in the breakdown! Working the Word gives us God's strength to overcome every challenge that rises up against us! You, too, are abundantly blessed—regardless of what life may look like right now. Choose to agree with God's plans for your abundance by saying the following declarations out loud, boldly and with confidence:

"I am abundantly blessed!"

"Abundance belongs to me because I have abundant favor with God!"

"There is abundant increase in my spiritual life!"

"There is abundant increase in my physical life!"

"There is abundant increase in my financial life!"

"There is an abundant increase in every area of my personal life!"

As you believe what God has said and begin to act on it, you will break through into new areas of abundance that are awaiting you.

START WHERE YOU ARE AND WORK WITH WHAT YOU HAVE

To quote a well-known adage, "There's no time like the present." Remember, we serve a "now" God, and if we choose to obey Him now, we can experience His blessings *now* as well. So many people are projecting their hopes and dreams into the future, but God is giving us the fulfillment of our hopes and dreams now—in the present. If we start where we are and begin working with what we have, we can see God do great things in our lives *right now*!

When I was a teenager, a visiting evangelist's message opened my spiritual eyes and heart to God's plan for abundance in a new and exciting way. Until that day, I had never heard about the principle of sowing and reaping or even about what it meant to be a good steward of my financial resources. No one at my church ever talked about money. So, when evangelist John Shiver preached on Jesus's parable of sowing and reaping and about multiplication, he encouraged the congregation to trust God regarding their finances. (See, for example, Matthew 13:3–22; 25:14–30; 2 Corinthians 9:6.)

I was so motivated by what the Word of God had to say about this "taboo" topic of money that I accepted it as truth, eager to see what my newfound understanding would yield. At the time, I taught cartooning art classes and was making $35 a week, which wasn't a lot but was adequate spending money for a teenager. The day the evangelist spoke, I had a $20 bill in my wallet that I was hoping would last until payday. But when the offering plate came to me, I put in the bill. I trusted that God would use the money for His glory and then multiply it back to me. I didn't know how it all worked, but I believed it would.

After church that evening, a couple of friends and I decided to go to a restaurant to hang out. By the time we arrived, I had received $60 from a completely unexpected source! In my spirit, I knew that God was providing an overflow of abundance in response to my obedience and commitment to His law of multiplication. I also knew that I was to share this blessing with my friends, so I bought all of our meals.

The lesson I learned that day became a way of life for me. When you work God's Word into your heart, His Word will work for you. I'm so thankful that the evangelist shared God's wisdom regarding finances—it has made a world of difference to me and to all those I've shared it with over the years. I pray the same for you. We will talk more about the spiritual art of sowing when we explore "Divine Mystery #4: What You Sow, You Will Grow."

A MIRACLE SEED PLANTED INTO MIRACLE SOIL WILL PRODUCE A MIRACLE HARVEST.

We move into God's abundance by allowing His abundance to move into us. God's ability to use what's in your hand is far greater than your ability to use what's in God's hand. What I mean is that God is the Master Multiplier. If we submit what we carry into His plans and purposes, we can see divine abundance and acceleration take place in amazing ways. Just consider what happens when you place a seed into the ground—the miracle of life takes root and starts to sprout up, and then fruitfulness begins! Similarly, the Spirit leads us to follow His guidance, and when we do, abundance appears on the scene.

Several years ago, my sister, Sabrina, and her husband were struggling financially. Both had full-time jobs, putting in many hours at the bank where they worked, trying to earn enough money to make ends meet. They were good at their jobs, and they were well-liked by their employers and coworkers, but finances were still tight.

When Sabrina was pregnant with their second child, the doctor prescribed bedrest for a month, allowing her time to prepare for the arrival of their daughter. During Sabrina's online shopping endeavors, she discovered a unique baby car seat cover. It was a clever three-in-one design that not only could be used as a shield to protect a baby from the elements but could also be used as a garment to cover the mother and baby during breastfeeding and as a protective cover for a shopping cart seat. It was ingenious! Sabrina purchased one, and, after the baby arrived, she began using it. When she visited us one day, Janet commented on how practical the baby cover was. At the time, Janet was expecting our daughter Legacy, so she asked Sabrina about making a homemade version of the item for her.

Within a few days, Sabrina began working on an even better-quality version of the car seat cover. She designed a new pattern, purchased the right fabric, and asked our grandmother for assistance in sewing several new covers. She made one for herself, one for us, and some for a few other friends. When she presented us with this gift, we marveled at how wonderful it was. Sabrina had taken an idea and allowed the Spirit to show her how to improve it, meeting a need for herself and others. Suddenly, Sabrina began receiving requests for the cover from people on social media and from other people who saw her using it as she traveled around town.

At first, our grandmother could keep up with the demand, sewing dozens of baby covers. But after several newspaper and magazine articles were written about Sabrina's baby-cover design, the orders multiplied to the point that Sabrina had to hire a team of seamstresses and other employees. Eventually, the baby cover was sold in stores across Canada and around the world—and it still is today. Each item is labeled with a special "Psalm 91" Scripture reminder, which has blessed countless lives. My sister and her family have been abundantly provided for by the Lord as they have grown their small business into a multimillion-dollar baby goods empire called The OVer Company. It is a true rags-to-riches story.

God knows what the future holds for you. Be open to His voice and His plans. Studying and reflecting on God's Word and receiving His revelation can solve the most profound mysteries and answer all of life's questions. What you glean from His Word will work wonders in your life—and will impact generations to come.

As I wrote in the preface, the Bible says that, as God's children, we can search out and understand His mysteries. (See Matthew 13:11.) Proverbs 25:2 teaches us, *"It is the glory of God to conceal a thing: but the honor of kings is to search out a matter."* And the book of Revelation tells us that God has made us to be kings and priests unto Him. (See Revelation 1:6; 5:10.) We are given the ability to dive into the Word and search out the mysteries of God.

In a brief moment, God can illuminate your understanding, and you will discern something very powerful in the realm of the Spirit. And when you see it, you can have it. Whatever you see in God now belongs to you; you can possess it. (Remember the first divine mystery—*heavenly vision is a pathway for provision*.)

WHATEVER GOD ALLOWS YOU TO SEE, YOU CAN HAVE!

THE WORD AND WORKING ANGELS

When God's mysteries unfold, we begin to view ourselves as He views us. His light shines on our way, and all His promises are now ours. This is a very supernatural and wonderful aspect of our lives as believers. In this book, I've been so excited to share with you various mysteries the Lord has unfolded to me through His Word—including the role of angels in our lives.

Psalm 91 is a wonderful song about David's experience in the secret place of God. It tells us much about the glory realm and living in that glory, as well as about the benefits, blessings, and favor we find when we position ourselves to live in God's manifest presence. When we do so, God lives through us to bless others.

The psalm also tells us about the angels God has assigned to us. Psalm 91:11 in the *New Living Translation* says it this way: *"For he will order his angels to protect you wherever you go."* God directs His angels to do various tasks on our behalf. They are His angels, His servants— and He gives them assignments to keep us safe in all our ways.

When you read Psalm 91:11, who do you think of when it says, *"He shall give His angels charge over **you**, to keep **you** in all your ways"*? Who is the *you* referred to here? If you're like me, when I read the Bible, I see myself in every verse. In my case, that *you* is ME! In your case, that *you* is YOU! You are the one to whom God has assigned angels. This is a revelation that each of us needs to understand and believe; and when you accept this revelation, you will begin to see life very differently.

Because God's angels are assigned to us, we could even call them *our* angels. There are angels surrounding you, and they have been ordered by God, specifically placed by Him, to help you with all of life's issues. You may not have seen them, felt them, or heard them, but they are there nevertheless. God said so, and He always does what He says.

If you have never seen angels, felt their presence, or heard their voices, I encourage you to open up your spiritual eyes, become more sensitive to their presence, and have a real-life encounter with them.[12] Let's ask God to make our spirits more discerning of what is happening around us. Let's ask Him to open our eyes a little wider. Let's ask Him to give us more sensitive ears. I believe God has a special revelation for His body of believers today. It is the revelation of the angelic realm around us and the benefits angels can bring to our daily lives.

I believe strongly that God wants His body, His sons and daughters, to become more aware of the angels He has assigned to assist them. There are entire armies of angels, the hosts of heaven, that are at our disposal. They are available and can be counted on to do whatever is necessary to further the purposes of God in our lives.

---

12. For more biblical teaching in this regard, see my book *Seeing Angels* (New Kensington, PA: Whitaker House, 2019).

I have written several books about angels and often speak on that topic because (1) God created angels for a purpose, and (2) many believers still have not grasped this truth. I've also conducted angel schools in many locations because I feel an urgency in my spirit at this particular moment in time for the body of Christ to awaken to all of the abundance that God has made available for us in the glory realm. As I mentioned previously, we look at the mystery of "Angel Power Makes Abundance Shower" in Divine Mystery #6.

A lot of angelic activity is recorded in the Bible, in both the Old and New Testaments, and I am convinced that God sends angels to assist us now as well—perhaps even more now than at any other moment in history. Some people might disagree, and that is their privilege. Some might believe that angels were primarily for Old Testament times because believers are now filled with the Holy Spirit and no longer require the aid of angels. After all, we have God in the form of the Holy Spirit living inside us. That's true, but the Holy Spirit is not just a replacement for the ministry of angels. The Holy Spirit is God, and He is infinitely higher than angels.

When God created angels, He had something very special in mind for them. The truth that the Holy Spirit came into the world and endued men and women with heavenly power does not mean that angels suddenly became meaningless or obsolete.

The reality is that more angelic activity is recorded in the New Testament than in the Old Testament. It is impossible to read the whole New Testament and miss that. In fact, there is more angelic activity recorded in the book of Revelation than in any other part of the Bible— and much of that book is just now being played out in our lives, with much more to come. This tells me that as we approach the final days of time, God is increasing our knowledge of and access to His holy angels. The ministry of angels is not disappearing—instead, it is being accelerated. As we approach the end, there will be a greater and greater release of God's angels upon the earth.

Note that while God's angels have a purpose, that purpose is *not* to be worshipped. They don't help us so that we will become obsessed with them or pray to them. They come to give God glory and to work with God's people to accomplish God's work. God's Word is a foundation we can all stand on and build on, and the writer of Hebrews declares, *"Are they* [angels] *not all ministering spirits, sent forth to minister for them who shall be heirs of salvation?"* (Hebrews 1:14). Some translations say, *"...those who will inherit salvation."* The meaning is the same.

The idea is that if you receive Jesus Christ into your heart, if you have accepted Him as your Lord and Savior, you inherit salvation and will live forever in heaven with Him. This is the only way you can get to heaven. You can't get to heaven just because you're a good person or do good things. The only way to the Father and the only way to enter heaven is by receiving Jesus Christ as your personal Lord and Savior. You need to say, "Jesus, I need You. I can't live without You. Because of Your sacrifice and the blood You shed, I am cleansed. I am purified. I am reconnected to Father God and given divine communion." When you sincerely pray that prayer, you are now positioned in the Spirit as an heir of salvation. How wonderful!

You are now royalty in the Spirit realm. If you don't understand that, you might walk around sad and depressed and live your daily life down-and-out. But when you recognize that when Jesus comes into your heart, He brings a supernatural change, it makes all the difference. He repositions you, takes you out of the kingdom of darkness— where you were bound, discouraged, depressed, in pain, and full of shame and guilt—and into the light, the kingdom of God. Here's how the Bible describes it:

> *Giving thanks to the Father...who has delivered us from the power of darkness, and has translated us into the kingdom of His dear Son.*
> (Colossians 1:12–13)

As a believer, you are no longer part of the kingdom of darkness. You are now part of the kingdom of light. You have moved into God's royal family. Let's pray together right now to establish this truth in our hearts and minds:

> O Lord, I thank You that we are now heirs of salvation. I thank You that we are royalty in the Spirit and that, as part of the royal family, the family of God, we have many benefits and

privileges. Thank You for Your Word, which works for all who believe! Amen.

RECEIVE THE WORD OF REVELATION

We all go through difficult experiences in life, walking out this journey of faith step-by-step. God wants us to keep moving into greater and greater life—abundant life. But we need His revelation before we can move into it. That revelation is God's gift to us, given through His Word and His Spirit, and it enables us to enter into the manifestation of what has been revealed. If we don't have the revelation, we can't demonstrate the reality of it.

For example, many wonderful believers—who are, without a doubt, saved—have never received a revelation about God's healing power. And because they have never received the revelation that God wants to heal them, they walk around defeated by pain and sickness. I'm not casting judgment on the sick; I'm just saying that there's something better. In the same way, many people have not yet received the revelation of God's abundant provision, which is an extension of Himself.

God gives us many powerful promises in the Bible. We need to remember that He created everything we see with the words He spoke at the very beginning of the world, and His words are still creating and restoring people and things today. He has revealed to us His delivering power so we can walk in freedom and cease being tormented by the enemy. God is everything we need, and in Him is everything we need. If we accept that revelation, heavenly abundance can manifest in our lives.

SEEK GOD'S REVELATIONS IN HIS WORD
ABOUT HEALING, PROVISION, POWER,
AND THE ANGELIC REALM.

WORD-BASED PRAISE LEADS TO REVELATION

When we read God's Word and meditate on His purposes, our response is to praise Him for His love and His works—and our praises can then lead to further revelation.

The psalmist David lived about a thousand years before the birth of Christ. During his youth, he was a humble shepherd boy. Often alone on the hills of Judea with his flocks, he loved to play his harp and sing songs of his love for God. The words of those songs still bless us today.

Think of Psalm 23, for example. Its words are so beautiful that they have been engraved and printed on plaques worldwide so people can continually be reminded of and encouraged by them. Psalm 23 hangs on the walls of many church nurseries, and most of us learned it in childhood. We have not only learned it, but we have also quoted it, sung it, and prayed it. But this psalm is not a cute children's verse. David realized that when he sang to God, there was power in his words of praise. When he praised God, something happened in the spiritual realm. In that realm, he could go places no one else was going.

Psalm 22 is another of David's songs of worship that he wrote with words from his heart. Beginning with verse 6, David sang these words:

But I am a worm and not a man, scorned by everyone, despised by the people. All who see me mock me; they hurl insults, shaking their heads. "He trusts in the LORD," they say, "let the LORD rescue him. Let him deliver him, since he delights in him." (Psalm 22:6–8 NIV)

Moving ahead to verse 12, David continues to sing to his Lord:

Many bulls surround me; strong bulls of Bashan encircle me. Roaring lions that tear their prey open their mouths wide against me. I am poured out like water, and all my bones are out of joint. My heart has turned to wax; it has melted within me. My mouth is dried up like a potsherd, and my tongue sticks to the roof of my mouth; you lay me in the dust of death. Dogs surround me, a pack of villains encircles me; they pierce my hands and my feet. (Psalm 22:12–16 NIV)

Surely this doesn't sound like a young shepherd boy surrounded by his sheep. Who was David talking about when he sang, *"They pierce my hands and my feet*"? That should be a clue. David didn't have his hands and feet pierced. So, it seems the words he wrote and sang were about the crucifixion of Christ. Yes, even a thousand years before it happened, David was singing about Jesus going to the cross. Through praise and worship, he had connected with the Spirit of God in such a way that he could transcend time and space and go somewhere he had never been.

The same experience happened to John the Revelator. He saw a heavenly door standing open and then heard a voice, like the blast of a trumpet, calling him, saying, *"Come up here, and I will show you what must take place after this"* (Revelation 4:1 NIV). That's how the Holy Spirit, the Spirit of Revelation, works. And when you begin to engage with the revelation of God, you will go places you've never been to, see things you've never seen, and receive things you've never had in order to do something that no one else has done.

God desires to bring manifestations to your life—manifestations of healing, manifestations of blessing, manifestations of goodness, manifestations of favor. He wants to release many kinds of manifestations, but they will only come as you allow the Spirit to bring you revelation. There are downloads of ideas, inventions, and creative abilities waiting for you in heaven. Will you receive these revelations and rise up into the Spirit realm to do new things?

Even though David was just a young shepherd, God showed him revelation, and, suddenly, he had eyes to see beyond his lifetime, eyes to see a thousand years into the future. It was as if David himself was witnessing the crucifixion through the eyes of Christ, for he seemed to write the words and sing what he was seeing in the first person. It was just that real to him:

> *A pack of villains encircles me; they pierce my hands and my feet. All my bones are on display; people stare and gloat over me. They divide my clothes among them and cast lots for my garment.*
> (Psalm 22:16–18 NIV)

For those who know the details of the crucifixion, you can't get more precise than that, and yet this event didn't take place until a thousand years later. Why do you suppose God would allow David to see the crucifixion? Let's look at Acts 2. Speaking of David, Peter preached:

> But he was a prophet and knew that God had promised him on oath that he would place one of his descendants on his throne. Seeing what was to come, he spoke of the resurrection of the Messiah, that he was not abandoned to the realm of the dead, nor did his body see decay. God has raised this Jesus to life, and we are all witnesses of it. Exalted to the right hand of God, he has received from the Father the promised Holy Spirit and has poured out what you now see and hear. For David did not ascend to heaven, and yet he said, "'The Lord said to my Lord: "Sit at my right hand until I make your enemies a footstool for your feet."'"
> (Acts 2:30–35 NIV)

"God has raised this Jesus to life, and we are all witnesses of it." Not only did David see Christ's crucifixion, but he also saw His resurrection, and that revelation changed David's inner self. What he began saying and writing from that point on was different from what anybody else had said to that point.

This brings us to Psalm 103, beginning with verse 1, which shows how David applied the revelation he had received about the Messiah: "Bless the LORD, O my soul: and all that is within me, bless His holy name." David was speaking to his soul—to his mind, as well as his emotions. He was speaking to "all" that was within him, and he was commanding it to bless the Lord and His holy name.

"Bless the LORD, O my soul, and forget not all His benefits" (Psalm 103:2). How did David know about the benefits of Calvary? He knew because the crucifixion and the resurrection had been revealed to him by the Spirit. Again, David knew something that other people didn't yet know, and it changed his life.

There are places in the Spirit where God wants to take you, and it will forever change you. It will change what you say and what you do. When you see a spiritual reality through the revelation of God's Word, you can have that reality—and that changes everything.

David became very bold with the words of this song:

Who forgives all your iniquities; who heals all your diseases; who redeems your life from destruction; who crowns you with lovingkindness and tender mercies; who satisfies your mouth with good things; so that your youth is renewed like the eagle's. (Psalm 103:3–5)

A thousand years before Jesus went to the cross, David already knew that God's Son would pay the price for our sins to be forgiven, that He would heal all our diseases, that He would redeem our lives from destruction, that He would crown us with lovingkindness and tender mercies, that He would satisfy our mouths with good things so that our youth is renewed like the eagle's. David foresaw all of these abundant benefits and blessings in the Spirit.

Let's look at one more verse from this psalm, a that Scripture we looked at in a previous chapter: *"Bless the LORD, you His angels, that excel in strength, that do his commandments, hearkening to the voice of His word"* (Psalm 103:20). First, David commanded his own soul to reverence God, and then he spoke directly to the angels of God and commanded them to do the same!

Remember what David wrote about angels in Psalm 91: God gives His angels charge over us to keep us in all our ways. We talked about how this is a personal promise for each of us. Now we see David actually commanding angels, and that was something that not many others were doing at the time. When you absorb the revelation knowledge of abundance flowing in your life, then you, too, will do things that others are not doing.

Now, let's prepare to unlock the fourth divine mystery—all about sowing and growing. Sooner than later, you will be reaping God's abundant blessings in every area of your life!

DECREES OF ABUNDANCE

As you decree the following truths, you can expect to manifest unlimited, overflowing abundance. Spirit, let it flow!

* *God's Word is lighting my path and watering my soul.*

- *I am moving into abundance according to God's Word.*

- *I do what God says, and I receive what God says.*

- *Abundance is coming to me NOW!*

- *Abundance belongs to me because I have abundant favor with God.*

- *I bless the Lord, and I receive all of His supernatural benefits.*

- *I am abundantly blessed!*

CHAPTER 5

DIVINE MYSTERY #4:
WHAT YOU SOW,
YOU WILL GROW

*"My **God shall supply all your need** according to
His riches in glory by Christ Jesus."*
—Philippians 4:19

The last time I checked, that promise in Philippians 4:19 had not changed. God hasn't run out of provisions. In fact, there is an overflowing abundance in the treasuries of heaven, and it is all accessible to us. God's treasures are available for the righteous, available for worshippers, available for those who will say, "Yes, Lord, I will respond to Your call. I will rise up and let my light shine. I will share the gospel. I will be a soul winner. I will be a miracle worker. I will do what You said I could do in this hour. I will rely on You, the Greater One inside me. You are greater than anyone or anything. You are greater than any recession or any sickness. You have already taken care of it. And if it's done, it's done!"

In John 19:30, Jesus said, *"It is finished"*—and it is. A few years ago, the Spirit spoke to me, "You've already won. When Jesus said, 'It is finished,' your problems diminished. You now have the victory. So, rejoice in that glory. Jesus paid the great price for you to now live in Christ. You can walk in realms of the divine supernatural." I keep declaring victory because of what Jesus did for us. I declare it over all the situations in my life.

You can too. When everything around you looks bleak, just say, "I'm going to let the Light that is within me overcome the external obstacles that surround me. God in me is greater than anything in this world." (See 1 John 4:4.)

In my book *31 Days to a Miracle Mindset*, I wrote, "Miracles do not always happen in the place where they are needed, but they always appear in the place where they are seeded." We see so many needs on the earth that it's often overwhelming, and we may wonder, "God, why are You not responding to us?" We must understand that miracles do not always occur where people need them—they happen where people plant seeds that will bear the fruit of a heavenly response.

In recent years, there have been many teachings in the church about the amazing potential of "planting a seed." But what kind of seeds does this principle apply to? A seed can be finances, time, words, labor, compassion, and much more. Basically, a seed is anything that multiplies when placed in the proper soil and atmosphere where it has the ability to flourish and create a harvest. A seed is intended to bring fruitfulness. God never gives us seed without expecting fruitfulness to come forth from it. A seed sowed and cared for will produce a bounty.

> MIRACLES DO NOT ALWAYS HAPPEN IN THE PLACE
> WHERE THEY ARE NEEDED, BUT THEY ALWAYS APPEAR
> IN THE PLACE WHERE THEY ARE SEEDED.

PLANTING OUR SEEDS FOR GOD'S GLORY

In chapter 1, where we discussed the biblical foundations of abundance, we recognized one of the first commands God gave to humankind:

Be fruitful and multiply....   (Genesis 1:28 NLT)

Our very lives are seeds, and everything God has given us are seeds with which to be fruitful and multiply. We need to ask ourselves, "What will I do with the seeds I have been given? Where will I sow these seeds?"

To help answer this question, let's look at some biblical examples of various spiritual seeds we can sow and the fruit they produce:

- *Honor* is a seed for longevity. (See Exodus 20:12.)

- *Communication* is a seed for understanding. (See Colossians 4:6.)

- *Kindness* is a seed for emotional and physical healing. (See Proverbs 16:24.)

- *Peace* is a seed for righteousness. (See James 3:18.)

- *Gratitude,* or *thankfulness,* is a seed that opens doors of opportunity. (See, for example, Psalm 100:4–5.)

- *Forgiveness* is a seed that produces peace. (See, for example, Hebrews 12:14–15.)

- *Financial sacrifice* is a seed that produces financial harvest. (See, for example, Luke 6:38.)

Here are some other seeds and their harvests that I have discovered:

Excellence is a seed for recognition, and *integrity* is a seed for promotion. When we sow a seed of integrity, it may not be noticed by other people. In fact, they may not even recognize that we have sowed it. But that seed of integrity will bring us into divine promotion. Always remember that God is the One who does the promoting. Therefore, it doesn't matter what other people see or don't see of our lives. All that matters is what God sees—and I can tell you with assurance that He sees everything. *Praise* is a seed for changing the atmosphere for spiritual victory. *Worship* is a seed for a cloud of glory. *Time* is a seed for eternity; God gives us our time to invest wisely in storing up treasures in heaven. (See Matthew 6:19–20.)

Action is a seed for success, and that's a revelation some people especially need to hear. Don't get me wrong. We all need periodic rest. And all of us need to soak in God's presence. Soaking in and soaking up the manifest presence of God is absolutely essential. We need to enter into the ease of the glory. But once we are in that glory, God gives us instructions about things that we are to *do*. It is good to spend time on the floor, humbled before God, but then, when His direction comes, we must get up off the floor and put our hands to the plow. God requires the work of our hands as much as He requires our devotion. Action is a major key to success, and if you're having difficulty with attaining success, the issue just might be that you're not taking action. Success is God's will for your life. It's what He has called you to enjoy. Are you allowing the Spirit to direct your steps? If you let Him, He will lead you into the divine place that brings you into divine success.

As you can see, there are various types of seeds that we can sow and grow. When you sow into the glory of God, it positions your heart in a place of trust. It's not about trying to move God's hand to bless you. He wants us to be blessed. He has already made up His mind to bless us, and this is His will for us. He loves to pour out goodness upon us. We, then, have the responsibility to do the right thing—to conduct our lives in a way that demonstrates that we trust Him. That is why seed sowing is so wonderful. It puts us in a place where we say, "God, I trust You more than I trust my money, my time, and my other resources. I trust You with everything."

PLANTING IN GOOD SOIL

Once, a woman asked me, "Why is it that I've been having a problem with my seed? I've been sowing, sowing, and sowing some more, but I have not seen a return." I asked her where she had been sowing, and she named a ministry that was very religious but had no manifestations of God's glory. "They're not Spirit-filled," she said, "but I thought I should sow my seed there because that's what I've always done."

"That might be your problem," I told her. "You may not be sowing into good soil. Your seed can be good, but if you're not sowing it into good soil, you can't expect much of a harvest. Just like any wise farmer, you need to be careful where you plant your seed."

In the parable of the sower, Jesus spoke about the importance of planting in good soil:

Then He spoke many things to them in parables, saying: "Behold, a sower went out to sow. And as he sowed, **some seed fell by the wayside***; and the birds came and devoured them.* **Some fell on stony places***, where they did not have much earth; and they immediately sprang up because they had no depth of earth. But when the sun was up they were scorched, and because they had no root they withered away. And* **some fell among thorns***, and the thorns sprang up and choked them. But* **others fell on good ground and yielded a crop***: some a hundredfold, some sixty, some thirty. He who has ears to hear, let him hear!"*   (Matthew 13:3–9 NKJV; see also Mark 4:1–20)

In this parable, four different types of soil are depicted. The first type of soil is described as *"the wayside,"* which speaks of the casual recipient, a person unwilling to receive God's Word with any depth of commitment. They can take the gospel or leave it. As a result, the seed sowed in their life is eaten up by other ideas and opinions they hold (or hear) that are not based on God's truth, and the seed quickly disappears from their life.

The second type of soil Jesus mentions is *"stony."* This kind of soil speaks of a doubtful receiver, and such a receiver also cannot produce a harvest. This person initially accepts the Word, but the seed only falls onto shallow soil in their life. The roots sprout and try to take hold, but they have no room to spread out and flourish. The moment any scorching trial comes along or any winds of uncertainty, their faith withers, and all hope of their having a harvest is gone.

The third type of soil is one inhabited with *"thorns,"* which speaks of the natural-minded recipient, a person who has a greater desire for earthly concerns than for heavenly priorities. The seed begins to grow but is choked by the adjacent thorns of the cares of life, having no chance to fully become established and draw in nutrients—and soon dies.

The fourth type of soil Jesus mentions is, of course, the ideal. *"Good ground"* is freshly tilled and free of rocks and weeds, and it represents the generous receiver of God's Word. I like to call this the "God soil"— and God soil brings forth a God harvest.

The soil Jesus spoke of can apply to people, places, or atmospheres. He said that His Word is the seed, and He gave examples of those who receive it but neglect it and suffer loss, and those who nourish it and allow it to flourish in their lives. Be careful where you sow your seed, realizing that the quality of the soil will either cause that seed to live or to die.

"GOD SOIL" BRINGS FORTH A GOD HARVEST.

GOD SOIL AND THE MIRACLE SEED

The Bible tells us that in the beginning, God brought forth man from the dust of the earth. (See Genesis 2:7.) He created "God soil" for the "God seed" that He was sowing. His plan was that human beings would have an abundant harvest in their lives—spiritual blessing, health, and prosperity in every way. Again, God soil with a God seed produces a God harvest. God soil is miracle ground that produces miracle results—wonderful fruitfulness and multiplication. Praise God! Isn't He awesome?

Always remember the Word of God is a miracle seed. Earlier, we talked about Galatians 6:7, which says, *"Do not be deceived, God is not mocked; for whatever a man sows, that he will also reap"* (NKJV). When you sow the Word of God, you will reap the harvest of that Word.

You can plant the Word of God as a miracle seed in your heart and then watch it grow. Over the days and weeks and months of the year in which we read the Bible, miracle seeds are being deposited into our spirits, and they are not placed there to die. They have not been planted there to get choked out by the cares of the world. God planted them with the anticipation of watching each one grow and flourish, providing a harvest in your life.

I enjoy reading from the *American Patriot's Bible* edition. One of the things I appreciate the most about America is its pioneering spirit. I love the American spirit that says, "Let's not wait for someone else to make it happen. Let's be the ones to make it happen. Let's just go and do it." I love these freedoms and liberties that release creative glory.

This Bible contains the following quote, which is attributed to George Washington, the nation's first president: "It is impossible to rightly govern the world without God and the Bible."[13] The seed of the Word was planted in America hundreds of years ago and was confirmed by the very first president.

Also in that Bible is this quote by John Quincy Adams, the sixth president: "The first and almost the only book deserving of universal attention is the Bible. I speak as a man of the world…and I say to you, 'Search the Scriptures.'"[14] Once again, the Word was a seed planted in America for an expected harvest.

And Abraham Lincoln, the sixteenth president of the United States, said, "In regard for this Great Book [the Bible], I have this to say, it is the best gift God has given to man. All the good Savior gave to the world was communicated through this Book."[15]

Yes, the Word is the best gift, the best seed. God watches over His Word and will fulfill it. (See Jeremiah 1:12.) Impartations of wisdom and revelation are released through the Word of God, impartations that come as the Word is continually deposited into our lives as seeds that grow abundant, nourishing fruit.

As I mentioned previously, when I was sixteen, I had a powerful encounter with the Holy Spirit. I was touched in a very personal way and began to experience God in a new light and in new dimensions I never even knew possible. Part of that touch was the Spirit guiding me to play the piano.

All I had to practice on was a very tiny keyboard. It was more of a toy than a real instrument. But when I sat down and began to play, the Spirit showed me what to do. I sat there for hours, singing songs to God. He was giving me a heart of worship. During that time, I fell in love with the Father, with Jesus, and with the Holy Spirit in a whole new way.

One evening, when I told my grandfather what was happening to me, he said, "I want to give you a book about real revival, true

---

13. Thomas Nelson, Inc., *The American Patriot's Bible: The Word of God and the Shaping of America*, ed. Dr. Richard G. Lee (Nashville, TN: Thomas Nelson, Inc., 2009), 181.
14. Ibid.
15. Ibid., 182.

revival." He went to his library and was gone for a little while. When he returned, he had in his hand a book entitled *Glory: Experiencing the Atmosphere of Heaven* by Ruth Ward Heflin. I had never heard of Calvary Campground in Ashland, Virginia, where Sister Ruth ministered, or her ministry in Israel, but I was eager to learn. He handed the book to me and said, "You need to read it." And I did. It's an amazing book, and it is especially important to me because it is the first book that was given to me after my initial encounter with the Spirit.

As I read *Glory*, I felt the Spirit stirring something inside me. I sensed the Spirit speaking to me through the black and white of those pages. I felt a spiritual impartation of the truths that Sister Ruth was sharing. Although she didn't know me, she was sowing seed into my life that has produced and reproduced continually over the years, providing spiritual fruit for many hungry people worldwide. Through the message of this book, I felt myself encountering the Holy Spirit again and again. For example, holy laughter would come over me, and sometimes I would "fall out" in my bedroom and just lie there in the presence of God's glory as He released His power to me.

We must realize that impartations can come to us not only directly through God's written Word, but also through people God uses to advance His kingdom message. *Impartation* is a seed, a miracle seed for a miracle harvest. If you have yet to read Ruth Ward Heflin's glory books, I encourage you to invest the money and time to read them.

THE POWER OF THE SEED

The next notable thing that happened to me occurred one day when I opened the pages of *Charisma* magazine and was immediately struck by a full-page ad that said, "Would you like to heal the sick?" I thought, "How awesome to be used to heal the sick!" I knew that we could pray for the sick because our church's weekly bulletin included a section citing the names of people who needed our prayers for healing. These people's names were also mentioned at some point during the Sunday service, and we asked God to heal them. Yet I couldn't help but notice that each week, the list was somewhat the same. The same people were still sick. Something about our remembering them was not working toward their healing.

Jesus was very specific with His disciples when He told them, *"Heal the sick"* (Matthew 10:8). And just before He returned to the Father, Jesus said, *"And these signs shall follow them that believe; in My name... they shall lay hands on the sick, and they shall recover"* (Mark 16:17–18). I didn't yet have that revelation.

The ad that had so moved me was from the ministry of Charles and Frances Hunter. They were offering a package of "How to Heal the Sick" books and VHS tapes—a video healing school course. I immediately knew that I wanted to get it.

I was still in high school, and it was a lot of money for me at the time, so I began to save my pennies, nickels, dimes, and dollars until I finally had enough to buy the whole package. I remember walking to the bank to get a money order and then placing it in an envelope and mailing it off. After that, I waited. I was so hungry for these teachings that it seemed like an eternity before the package finally came. The day it arrived, I was so excited. I opened it and began to devour every one of the resources. For an entire weekend, I was immersed in those books and recorded teachings. I couldn't wait to get started healing the sick.

I knew the Bible says we can't be just hearers of the Word, but we must also be doers, so I looked for opportunities to do what the books said I could do. It was so amazing! God began healing sick people through me. He released the Spirit's power for healing through my hands. Just as it was in the ministry of Jesus, healing became a great part of my ministry.

I have never forgotten how God can use resources—books, CDs, DVDs, and so forth—that honor and expound His Word as a means of imparting blessings to others. Someone who has already experienced God's gifts and power can then impart them. This is the main reason I have written so many books and released so many digital recordings focused on the supernatural power of God's glory. I want *every* believer to receive an impartation of the glory realm. As I share with you what I have learned and experienced in the Spirit, my prayer is that you will receive an impartation to carry this message and anointing farther than I can. This is the power of the seed. What you sow, you will grow!

Many years ago, the Lord directly spoke to Janet and me, saying, "What are you doing with the revelation I've given to you? Will you be good stewards of it? Release the things I have given to you—the revelations, the prophetic insights, the glory realm testimonies, the signs and wonders. Impart them to other believers, who will then release them to others." As we have discussed, people usually think of stewardship in regard to their finances alone, but God really wants us to steward our entire lives, allowing Him to "spend us" in any way He sees fit, using our anointings to bless others.

Sowing seed is a mandate we have received from God. We must not hold back. We can't be a one-person show, doing it all and keeping it all for ourselves; we must say, "Yes, God, I will release what I have so that others can also function in this gifting, so that others can operate in this ministry, so that others can do what You have shown us." And that is exactly what we have done!

It gives us great joy to sow cases of our books into the lives of young ministers and others who are being raised up in the Spirit. We often send cases of *Moving in Glory Realms* to Bible schools and training programs because it is a wonderful foundational book for those who desire more of God and those who need a strong biblical foundation for growing in the glory realm. We also sow our books to ministries in overseas nations, equipping them in the Word and in the Spirit. This is how we've learned to scatter our seed.

GOD WANTS US TO STEWARD OUR ENTIRE LIVES, ALLOWING HIM TO "SPEND US" IN ANY WAY HE SEES FIT, USING OUR ANOINTINGS TO BLESS OTHERS.

But books are not the only seed we sow. We also sow our time, our finances, and many other resources. Here is another supernatural secret that you must establish in your life, one that I introduced previously but is essential to truly understand: *you must sow whatever you desire to grow*. Write that statement down and remember it because it is an important spiritual principle.

For example, if you desire a financial harvest, you must sow a financial seed. Again, many believers are fearful of speaking about money because they have the wrong perspective about it, thinking the subject is taboo or that the Bible says money is the root of all evil. But that is incorrect. The Bible tells us that the *love of* money is what is wrong:

> For **the love of money is the root of all evil**: *which while some coveted after, they have erred from the faith, and pierced themselves through with many sorrows.*   (1 Timothy 6:10)

The Reverend Billy Graham wrote, "If a person gets his attitude toward money straight, it will help straighten out almost every other area of his life."[16] If we get our attitude about finances properly aligned, we can be positioned to use money as a miracle seed for manifesting abundance in every area of our lives. For far too long, many believers have had the wrong attitude about money and financial giving. In our church services, when offerings are received, some people think that the leaders are trying to take something from them. But that is the wrong perspective. Whenever we're presented with an opportunity to give, it is really an opportunity to be blessed. It is an opportunity to participate in something greater for God's glory, and an opportunity to plant a seed for a harvest for ourselves and others.

FIVE SUPERNATURAL SECRETS ABOUT MONEY

The following are five supernatural secrets for using money as a powerful seed, and ways you can manifest abundance.

1. MONEY IS AN IMPORTANT RESOURCE

Money is an important resource that God wants us to have so that His blessings can flow to us and through us. This resource enables you and me to do the things God has called us to do. Therefore, money should magnify the purposes of God in our lives.

> The rich rules over the poor, and the borrower is servant to the lender.   (Proverbs 22:7)

---

16. Billy Graham, *Unto the Hills: A Daily Devotional* (Nashville, TN: Thomas Nelson, 2010), May 5.

Today God is looking for those in the body of Christ whom He can raise up as possessors of great wealth. Why? So they can use their finances as a resource for kingdom glory, for kingdom harvest, for spreading the gospel, for souls, for miracles. He doesn't want us to be in debt or spread so thin financially that we can't provide for our needs or the needs of others.

Some believers say, "You don't seem to understand how dangerous money is! When people come into money, they change. They lose their devotion to God and start living for themselves." Again, it comes down to our attitude, which we need to establish in the truth so that we have the right perspective about the money we receive from God. The Bible does warn those who are wealthy to be generous and not to place their riches above their love for God. (See Matthew 19:16–30; 1 Timothy 6:17–18.) However, I don't believe people essentially change when they come into money—it just exposes what has been in their heart all along.

Some of the most generous people I've ever met were those who gave the last five, ten, or twenty dollars they had. It was all the money they possessed, and yet they said, "God, I want to give this to the work of the ministry." Those are the ones God loves to bless with thousands of dollars, tens of thousands of dollars, hundreds of thousands of dollars, and more. When they have their thousands and are generous with it, it reflects what is in their heart—magnified. It may look like they are now more generous givers, but the truth is that they have been generous all along the way. People who are generous with a little become generous when they have a lot.

I have also met people who are millionaires but live a very stingy lifestyle. When they go out to dinner with a group, they pay only for themselves or even expect someone else to pay for them. They have a greedy spirit. I have also known people who went from being millionaires to having nothing—and nothing about their attitudes really changed. They were selfish when they had a lot, and they are selfish now when they have only a little.

Again, money doesn't change people. It only magnifies what's already in their hearts. Will you consider your own attitudes toward money and how you can use your money as a resource to bless others?

2. MONEY IDENTIFIES THE TRUE LOCATION OF THE HEART

The Bible tells us that there is a correlation between the "location" of our money and the true attitude of our hearts. You will only invest in something you believe in. I encourage you to write this down: **I invest in what I believe in.**

If you invest in what you believe in, and you find yourself investing in God's kingdom, that's a sign you believe in what God is doing in the divine supernatural realm. Jesus told us, *"For where your treasure is, there will your heart be also"* (Matthew 6:21).

Does your heart align with what you say are your priorities? Another way of expressing this idea is, "Put your money where your mouth is." Some people talk really big, but when it comes to action, they rarely act on what they say. God wants us to be a people of our word so that we will do what we say and say what we do.

Are you investing in heavenly treasures?

3. MONEY SHOULD ALWAYS BE USED TO SERVE GOD

Your money should be used to serve God in *everything*. If you are not serving God by how you spend your money, it's time to reevaluate your spending. The next time you pay your bills or review your credit card statement, consider whether there is something you are spending money on that is not serving God, something He would not be pleased with. Taking care of your children is serving God, and it pleases Him. Paying your home loan or rent so that you can have a safe and secure place to live where you can practice hospitality is serving God, and it pleases Him.

Also consider what you are giving to your church and other ministries. When you go to church and give your offering, don't just be a "bucket plunker." Determine to serve God with your finances. Worship the Lord with your giving. The foolish serve themselves with money, but the wise serve God with their finances, realizing that He is the Source of overflowing abundance.

Personally, I want to go into deeper and deeper realms of true abundance, not for my own gain, but because I see the problems in our world, and I feel the heartbeat of God for humanity. God has given me a vision for a harvest of souls. I see that the needs are great in the nations of the earth, and I desire to enter into true abundance so God's blessings will flow to me and then flow through me to help others. And God wants you to enter into the realms of true abundance too.

When I speak of these blessings flowing to us, I want to emphasize again that this is not about having a dozen luxury cars in your driveway and swimming pools in the backyards of your four mansions. I'm not talking about stockpiling "things." If you have the mansions, the swimming pools, and the luxury cars, and God has given you the gift of hospitality, and you bless a lot of people through sharing those gifts, I think it's wonderful.

But let's remind ourselves of what true prosperity is because this term has been misused and misunderstood. From what I've learned through reading God's Word, prosperity is having enough to meet our own needs, with enough left over to be generous with others. Your own needs must be met before you can do what God has called you to do. Again, the calling of God on *your* life is different from the calling of God on *my* life, and it is different from the callings on your parents' lives, your children's lives, and your friends' lives. You have a special calling from God, and He desires to meet *your* needs. I encourage you to establish yourself in the following truth, which I've chosen as our chapter verse:

> *My God shall supply all your need according to His riches in glory by Christ Jesus.*   (Philippians 4:19)

Divine abundance is available to flow to you to meet your needs and equip you for your mission. But God doesn't just give you barely enough to meet those needs. The Bible declares that He is El Shaddai. Remember that this title means He is the God of more than enough. Oh, I like that!

Some people have experienced *enough,* and sadly, some have experienced *not enough* and *not even close to enough.* But God is the God of more than enough. When true abundance flows into your life, that is El Shaddai appearing on the scene and revealing His glory for all to see. Why? Because He is not a God of limited reserves and does not have just a trickling of riches. He is the God of more than enough for each and every one of us—if we will only hear the revelation, obey the revelation, and then receive the impartation of it.

Financial investments in the glory realm are the only ones guaranteed to never fail financially. The Bible talks about laying up treasures in a place where moth and rust cannot destroy them:

> Don't store up treasures here on earth, where moths eat them and rust destroys them, and where thieves break in and steal. Store your treasures in heaven, where moths and rust cannot destroy, and thieves do not break in and steal.... No one can serve two masters. For you will hate one and love the other; you will be devoted to one and despise the other. **You cannot serve God and be enslaved to money**.
>
> (Matthew 6:19–20, 24 NLT)

You cannot serve both God and money. This verse is speaking to us about a spirit of greed. You cannot serve God while, at the same time, serving a spirit of greed. God is not greedy; He's the opposite of greedy. He is generous; He gives on every occasion. God is continually giving out. Why do I say this? The book of Revelation portrays the realm of God's glory as a river. A river is continually moving, continually flowing, continually giving forth. Revelation teaches us that everywhere the river flows, there is life. On each side of this river, there is flourishing. There is harvest. There is fruitfulness. (See Revelation 22:1–2.) Let the abundant river of the Spirit's generosity flow into your life!

WHEN TRUE ABUNDANCE FLOWS INTO YOUR LIFE, THAT IS EL SHADDAI APPEARING ON THE SCENE AND REVEALING HIS GLORY FOR ALL TO SEE.

4. MONEY IS A TOOL FOR GLOBAL HARVEST

God is ready and able to reap a greater harvest in the earth as you financially invest in the salvation of souls, the miracle of healing, and the advancement of the good news of the gospel. Let's look further at what Paul wrote about God's provision in Philippians 4:

> *Now you Philippians know also, that in the beginning of the gospel,*
> *when I departed from Macedonia, no church communicated with*
> *me **as concerning giving and receiving**, but you only. For even*
> *in Thessalonica **you sent once and again to my necessity**. Not*
> *because I desire a gift: but I desire fruit that may abound to your*
> *account. But I have all, and abound: **I am full, having received** of*
> *Epaphroditus **the things which were sent from you,** an odor of a*
> *sweet smell, **a sacrifice acceptable, well pleasing to God**. But*
> *my **God shall supply all your need according to his riches in***
> ***glory by Christ Jesus.*** (Philippians 4:15–19)

Too often, we have not realized that the promise of overflowing abundance that Paul tells us about in Philippians 4:19 is directly connected to what comes before it. Our being able to receive from the heavenly realm is related to our being willing and able to give from what we have. We give from what we have to receive from what God has.

5. MONEY ALWAYS EXPOSES A POVERTY SPIRIT

One of the reasons many believers resist talking about money, listening to teaching about money, receiving money, and/or investing their finances in the kingdom is that an evil spirit of poverty is at work in an attempt to keep God's people bound in chains of lack. This spirit doesn't want believers to know what we discussed earlier in this book—that God is the One who gives us the ability to become prosperous:

> *And you shall remember the LORD your God, for it is He who gives*
> *you power to get wealth, that He may establish His covenant which*
> *He swore to your fathers, as it is this day.* (Deuteronomy 8:18 NKJV)

God has given us the ability to produce wealth—the gifts that will enable us to prosper and the resources to obtain and use financial blessings. He gives us the capacity and opportunities to enter into divine, supernatural abundance. God does this for us to confirm His covenant with our forefathers in the faith.

Although a poverty spirit still holds a number of people in bondage, as I have ministered worldwide in various regions over the past decade or so, I've noticed that the revelation of giving and the importance of generosity has taken root and is bearing fruit. This teaching is overtaking every area of the daily life of many believers. God's sons and daughters have become some of the most generous individuals I have ever met. This change has even occurred in places where the people previously had a deep-seated mentality of hoarding, stockpiling, and being independent, always trying to fend for themselves. Suddenly, they have become very generous, and God has been blessing them with riches. Only the glory of God can transform hearts and open up minds to receive the truth of God's Word. The glory creates an atmosphere where the seed can supernaturally be received.

The moment a poverty spirit is broken in someone's life by giving, a light comes on in their heart. The illumination of heaven comes and suddenly rises up. This light produces generous and genuine givers. If you are in this light, no one can tell you it doesn't pay to give to God because you know deep inside that He is worthy of every gift. You are a giver. Your spirit is generous, and in everything you do and at every opportunity, you are blessed. You are blessed to be a blessing. There is a miraculous overflow of abundance in your life that comes from heaven.

When a poverty spirit is exposed in the realm of your giving, it often shows itself in your receiving as well. This is evident when God wants to bless you, and you say something like, "Oh, no. I couldn't receive that." For instance, someone may say, "I'd like to pay for your meal," but you respond, "I'm fine, thank you. I've got it." When someone wants to bless you, allow them to do that. Don't allow the spirit of poverty or pride to keep you from receiving.

Additionally, too many believers keep it quiet and don't testify of God's great faithfulness when someone blesses them with finances. They worry about what others will think about them. If someone were to bless you with a new car, would you keep it a secret? Would you be concerned about people thinking a Christian or a minister shouldn't drive down the road in such a nice car? That's a spirit of poverty trying to attach itself to your ability to receive.

Concerning generous giving, the Bible says, *"Remember this—a farmer who plants only a few seeds will get a small crop. But **the one who** *plants generously will get a generous crop"* (2 Corinthians 9:6 NLT). The problem is that we too often concentrate exclusively on the part about bountiful *sowing* and ignore the part about bountiful *reaping*. Most of us look at the giving end, but there *is* a promise attached to it: *"the one who plants generously will get a generous crop."*

Whoever sows will reap, and whoever sows bountifully will reap bountifully. Therefore, don't be surprised when you sow bountifully and God's bountiful blessings are released into your life. Don't be surprised when a miracle flow of unlimited favor begins to overtake you. Don't be surprised when you see unlimited blessings and unusual abundance show up in your life. And whatever you do, don't resist the blessing.

The Bible makes it very clear that God has called you to be a blessing to others. How can you be a blessing if you are in desperate need yourself? How can you bless others when you constantly refuse the blessings God wants to release through you? May God give us an ear to hear what He is saying to His people.

God is looking for believers who will rise up and declare, "Father, I will be a generous giver. And Father, I will be a generous receiver so that I can continually be a generous giver. I realize that You have positioned me as a portal of heavenly glory here on earth. You desire to use me. You desire to release Your miracles in and through me so that others will come to know the revelation of Your goodness, the revelation of Your blessings, the revelation of Your abundance. Yes, God, I will be a generous giver, and therefore I will be a generous receiver. I won't give merely out of tradition, ritual, or habit. I won't give just because someone told me to do it. Your Spirit of generosity has risen inside me, and when that Spirit of glory flows, the generosity of the heavens is available to bring forth abundance not just for my need but also for the needs of others. I thank You for Your generous Spirit in me."

This realm of God's abundant overflow is not limited to your bank account. It's not governed by the local or national economy. This abundance flows from heaven, the realm of supernatural riches and treasures. God's realm of glory opening over you will enable you to preach the gospel with boldness. It might just launch you into the mission field, taking you to the nations. It will cause divine miracles and super-natural signs and wonders to be released.

Today, God desires to position you for abundance. He will not close the heavens to your pleas. But you must participate, cooperating with the heavenly realm. You must listen to God's instructions and be obedient to what He is saying. Position yourself in alignment with the open heavens, with the free-flowing river that comes forth from the throne of God.

Tell God now, "I will be open, just as You are open. I will be gen-erous, just as You are generous. I will do something I've never done before because I believe I will see something I've never seen before. I will follow You truly. I will look to Your ways. I will model my life after the life of Jesus. I will be an imitator of Christ. I will do what He did, operating in the same supernatural realm, living in the same abundant flow of the Spirit."

Let me remind you that when you determine to be open as God is open, this does not just mean having the openness to give but also having the openness to receive. I love what Isaiah 60:1 says. It has been my life's guiding revelation:

Arise, shine; for your light is come, and the glory of the LORD *is risen upon you.*

There is a vibrant, visible, and tangible glory arising upon the body of Christ today. Some believers have said to me, "But, Joshua, Isaiah 60:1 is a prophetic word for Israel." Yes, it is, but when God gives it to you, you can receive it with a grateful heart. I choose to take that word, to rise up and experience it. I will rise and shine, for my light has come, and the glory of the Lord has risen upon me. That choice to rise and shine is yours too.

This passage goes on to say:

For, behold, the darkness shall cover the earth, and gross darkness the people: but **the LORD shall arise upon you, and His glory shall be seen upon you.** *And* **the Gentiles shall come to your light,** *and kings to the brightness of your rising.*   (Isaiah 60:2–3)

The brilliance of God's glory will be seen in this world, and if you believe this and act on it, that brilliance will be seen upon you.

Then, Isaiah 60:11 says,

> **Your gates will always stand open**, *they will never be shut, day or night, so that* **people may bring you the wealth of the nations**—*their kings led in triumphal procession.* (NIV)

This is a promise from God. You are the greatest power portal of heavenly glory the earth will ever know. Your door will always stand open. Why? So that *"the abundance of the sea"* (Isaiah 60:5) and *"the wealth of the nations"* can be brought to you. When we open ourselves up to give, we position ourselves for abundance, saying, "God, I'm open to give, and as I do, I'm open to receive." When you do that, you can be sure that something miraculous is coming your way.

AN IMPARTATION FOR SOWERS

Right now, I want to release to you an impartation for sowing. I am not there to lay hands on you, but God is there with you. If you want a miracle impartation, He is with you to give it. If you desire to have a flourishing harvest in your life, He can do it for you. Open your heart, ready to receive what God gives. If you need healing in your body, financial provision, a breakthrough in a relationship, a resolution to a family matter—if you need restoration of any kind in your life or justice to be served for you or yours—let the abundance of God be released in your life and let it flow through you this day.

> Lord, I pray for Your glory to come to this reader. In Your glory is all that we need. Your glory is the essence of Your presence, Your character, Your nature. It is who You are. It is Your abundance. We have many specific needs, but in Your glory, all are met. We are hungry for Your blessings, and we receive Your glory. Amen!

How exciting that you have learned so much about God and yourself in the first four divine mysteries that unlock His unlimited abundance in the spiritual, financial, physical, relational, and vocational realms. Now you know for certain that He is ready, willing, and able to give you abundance. You are ready to enter into the next divine mystery: generous believing produces generous receiving!

DECREES OF ABUNDANCE

As you decree the following truths, you can expect the overflowing abundance of the Lord's goodness to be revealed in every aspect of your life. Spirit, let it flow!

- *The Spirit of abundance has reshaped the way I act and react to finances.*

- *Because I live in abundance, I always have more than enough supply.*

- *I am a child of God; I am a child of abundance.*

- *God has given me the ability to succeed and prosper in all that I do.*

- *I am well provided for—and I can provide well for others because abundance overflows in my life.*

- *I carry abundance, and I am able to release abundance to others.*

- *The Spirit of abundance is working in me on a daily basis.*

CHAPTER 6

DIVINE MYSTERY #5: GENEROUS BELIEVING PRODUCES GENEROUS RECEIVING

*"**Give, and it will be given to you.** A good measure, pressed down, shaken together and running over, will be poured into your lap. For with the measure you use, it will be measured to you."*
—Luke 6:38 (NIV)

When many Christians hear this passage from Luke 6 read at church, they get nervous because they are sure the preacher is about to take another offering and tell them they need to give more. If you think that's all Luke 6 is about, you are greatly mistaken and have not yet caught the revelation of what this Scripture is saying.

Luke 6:38 does say, *"Give,"* but only once. There are actually seven levels of supernatural receiving found within this verse, which we will examine later in this chapter. This Scripture is about positioning us to receive the greater glory and abundance of God. It is about positioning us to become generous *receivers*. Does that sound good to you? If so, let's take a closer look.

The passage begins with the challenge to give, but then it tells us what happens when we do. What we have given will be returned to us. Some people believe that when you give, you should say goodbye to your gift because it will go far, far away, and you will never see it again. But that is not what the Scripture says. It says that if you give, what you give will be given back to you. In other words, what you release comes back like a boomerang to your life. What you give comes right back to you.

Giving and then generously receiving from God's abundance go hand in hand. Actually, there is an art to receiving generously and graciously, which I will explain shortly. Too many Christians begrudgingly dwell on giving and sadly miss out on the promise of receiving.

Think about it! Abba Father desires for you to have every good thing He has prepared for you. He wants you to receive all of His blessings into your life. He tells you how to do this through the scriptural principles He reveals in His Word. These principles are a sort of protocol of the Spirit that positions you to come into the fullness of what has been supernaturally made available to you.

WHEN YOU GIVE, YOUR GIFT WILL BE RETURNED TO YOU.

When I travel the world to minister, my wife, Janet, often has to stay behind to care for our children and attend to the home front. When I'm away from my family, I think about them constantly; and everywhere I go, I look for something special to take back for them.

Also, when I travel, people frequently give me little gifts for our children—knickknacks, stuffed toys, candy, all sorts of things. When I get home, one of my favorite moments is when I pull into the driveway and see the front door open and hear our daughters scream, "Daddy! Daddy! Daddy!" Then there are lots of hugs. Janet is kind enough to allow them the first hug, but she's always waiting, too, and I look forward to her embrace.

The hugs and giggling and smiles are followed by the girls looking up at me with their big eyes and saying, "Daddy, did you get us something?" They know I always do. It so blesses my heart. I'm always delighted that they know when Daddy shows up, there will be blessings. When Daddy shows up, they will be loved on. When Daddy shows up, there will be gifts. When Daddy shows up, something good is going to happen. I love it.

Sometimes, they try to guess where the surprises are. "Daddy, is it in your shoulder bag? Or is it in that suitcase over there?" They really want to know where the blessings are, and, of course, that tickles me. Children are so cute and so wonderful.

In the same way, we need to realize that God takes joy in blessing us and know that He is delighted when we trustfully expect Him to give to us out of His abundance.

RECEIVE HIS ABUNDANCE

Growing up in the church, I heard people say phrases that, although they were probably originally spoken with good intentions, became distorted over the years. One of those phrases was, "Seek God's face, not His hand." There is a partial truth there. Yes, we want to seek the face of Jesus at all times, to look toward Him, to focus on Him—but, too often, that phrase has hindered people from moving into receiving all the gifts God has for them. They are afraid to seek the blessing of His hand.

What if my children were taught that philosophy and took it to heart? The arriving-home scene would be very different. After they ran to me and screamed, "Daddy, Daddy, Daddy," and we hugged and laughed and were so happy to see each other, I would say, "I have gifts for you!" But in this scenario, if they had been taught not to expect gifts from their father, they would say, "Oh, but Daddy, we just want to look at your face." Hmmm, that is not the response I would expect or even want.

I can't imagine saying, "Okay, that's fine. Just look at my face." Rather, I'd repeat, "I have gifts for each of for you! I want you to know I thought about you while I was gone, and I have gifts that I chose especially for you."

Yet, again, they would say, "But Daddy, we really just want to look at your face, not your hand."

And again I would respond, "But I got you some gifts you're really going to like. I was thinking about you when I saw them and knew you would love to have them. I really want to see the looks on your faces when I give them to you. I know they're going to be a blessing."

If they still refused to accept the gifts, I might start to wonder what Janet had been feeding these girls while I was away!

When our Father God, our Daddy, wants to give us something, we should get excited! And we should never feel bad when we're excited about what Daddy wants to give us. After all, we're not forcing Him to do it. We're not twisting His arm. He says He wants to give it to us. And if He wants to give it, we should be happy and thankful to receive it!

Why does God want to bless you? It's because He has been thinking about you all along and has prepared the blessing just for you. Don't you realize that when Jesus Christ hung on the cross of Calvary, when He suffered the pain and agony, bled, and died, He was thinking about you? If He had not been thinking about you, He never would have gone to the cross.

On the third day, Jesus rose again and now holds in His hand *"the keys of hell and of death"* (Revelation 1:18). Jesus didn't make His sacrifice in order to prove anything to Father God. He did it to reconcile you with God. He *gave* Himself for you. He did it because He cares for you, because He loves you. He suffered and gave His life because He wants to forgive you and give you eternal life.

Jesus's gift of Himself on our behalf brings abundance beyond our comprehension—and the descriptions of His blessings are found throughout the pages of the Bible. I heard someone say there are 365 different Scriptures about blessings in the Bible. That's one blessing for every day of the year. That sounded so good that I began to do some research and found that there are actually *more than* 365 Scriptures that speak of God's blessings for you and me—many for each day of the year—an abundance of blessings.

GOD'S ULTIMATE GIFT TO YOU IS JESUS—RECEIVE HIM WITH A GRATEFUL HEART.

Out of the overflow of God's love for you, He wants to shower you with abundance. I urge you to accept His gifts with joy, praise, and thanksgiving.

First John 5:5 says, *"Who is the one who is victorious and overcomes the world? It is **the one who believes** and recognizes the fact that Jesus is the Son of God"* (AMP). If we believe this foundational truth of the faith that Jesus is God's only Son, then we must also receive this truth and accept the victorious, abundant, overcoming life that He offers. I believe, and I have received. Have you?

SEVEN LEVELS OF SUPERNATURAL RECEIVING

Now let's look closely at the seven levels of supernatural receiving that Jesus spoke about in Luke 6:38:

Give, and it will be given to you. A good measure, pressed down, shaken together and running over, will be poured into your lap. For with the measure you use, it will be measured to you. (NIV)

LEVEL 1: "GIVE, AND IT WILL BE GIVEN TO YOU"

Luke 6:38 shows us how we can cooperate or partner with the Spirit to bring abundance into our daily lives. As we begin to release our resources to God, a supernatural release returns to us from heaven. Again, when you give, what you give will be returned to you. I don't see any loss in that. I don't see any lack in that. What you have given comes right back to you. Sometimes it returns in ways we expect, and other times God gives us supernatural surprises.

For example, Heather from New Zealand wrote to me after our ministry trip to Auckland. She shared, "We have appreciated the ministry you brought to us last month and we are learning to be generous receivers. God is surprising us with His provision in all sorts of ways. Including me going to the supermarket and finding, attached to the tray of eggs which I went to purchase, a note saying, 'Keep me.'

Taped to the note was a $5 bill." This unexpected blessing became a great encouragement to her. She knows that God sees us and that He cares about every little detail of our lives. Get ready to receive small gifts, medium-sized gifts, and large gifts from heaven—this is the way abundance works.

Many people have shared testimonies with us about the supernatural money miracles God gave them after they chose to sow into the glory realm. For example, Latoya in El Paso, Texas, said, "I sowed into the glory realm my very last $100, but the next morning my checking account had an unexpected $630! The very next morning!" This takes us to the next level of generous receiving: good measure.

LEVEL 2: "GOOD MEASURE"

"Good measure" signifies more than you gave in the first place. It indicates an increase. God has destined you for good measure. Although this principle can be applied to our finances, it can also be applied to the tangible, the physical, and every other way. Good measure can most certainly be applied to spiritual blessings and to soul blessings for your mind, your will, and your emotions. It applies to every area of your life!

Keep in mind what John wrote to the churches about prosperity: *"Beloved, I pray that **in every way you may succeed and prosper** and be in good health [physically], just as [I know] your soul prospers [spiritually].* (3 John 1:2 AMP). God desires to bless you in every possible way.

I urge you to realize today how much abundant overflow God wants to bring into your life. Again, this is not about heaping up material wealth or developing a materialistic or greedy mentality. This is not about hoarding. This is about having all that you need for yourself and being in a position to bless others. God wants to bless you so that you can be a blessing.

You and I must come to understand the pattern of God's kingdom. It is sowing and reaping, giving and receiving. A circle or flow is created in the Spirit realm that brings a constant stream of blessing your way. You can't give something you don't have. You can only release what you have first received. God wants to take you into a supernatural flow in order to carry you into the higher realms of His blessing.

You will be receiving abundance, and then you will be releasing abundance upon others. In other words, your life will become an open conduit through which the Spirit of generosity can flow.

What happens when the Spirit of generosity shows up? The spirit of poverty is instantly eliminated. Whenever and wherever the Spirit of generosity comes on the scene, the spirit of lack and insufficiency instantly disappears.

I have seen what a spirit of poverty can do to a church, to a family, or to a region—and it's not very nice. Far too many people have been taught that in order to be more holy or saintly, they have to be poor and live without. You must believe that living in constant lack is not God's plan for your life. That thought came from the enemy spirit. The spirit of poverty is absolutely devilish. It brings death, tragedy, heartache, famine, disease, and much more. So many horrible things are connected with that spirit, and God doesn't want you to connect with or have any part of it.

Our God is the Spirit of Generosity, and He wants the realm of His abundance to flow in and through your life every day. No matter what you do, no matter what you put your hands to, He wants to bless you so you can be a blessing.

LEVEL 3: "PRESSED DOWN"

The third level of receiving from God is *"pressed down."* There is a place in God where you can receive compacted abundance. This is not just the increase. This is increase pressed down. All the air pockets have been released from it. Therefore, it is one of the weightiest possible blessings you can be given.

One Hebrew word translated as "glory" is *kabod*, which literally means "weight."[17] This level of blessing from God is so weighty that you will feel the intense pressure of just how much He loves you and cares for you. Without a doubt, you will know that you are blessed by the Lord.

Recently, Janet and I went on a wonderful ministry trip with our two girls. We initially flew to West Palm Beach, Florida, and from there we rented a car and drove state by state to each location where

---

17. *Strong's*, #3519.

we would minister. When we started out, we had four suitcases, one for each of us. I asked the girls to pack lightly, anticipating receiving a few gifts that people usually give us. By the time we reached our second stop in Birmingham, Alabama, we had been so overwhelmingly blessed that our suitcases were packed to the brim, and we couldn't fit anything else into our rental car!

When we arrived at our next stop in Nashville, Tennessee, we had to upgrade our rental for a much larger vehicle. We stopped a few more times on the trip, visiting Jonesboro, Arkansas; Branson, Missouri; Tulsa, Oklahoma; Dallas, Texas; and Bourg, Louisiana. In each place we visited, the Lord put it on people's hearts to bless us with a variety of gifts.

One dear brother in the Lord came to a meeting with a juice blender in a box, saying that the Lord had instructed him to sow it into our lives. It was so refreshing to see such willing obedience to an unusual request from God. A few days later, at another church in another state, Janet felt led to give the blender away. I took it inside the church and surprised someone with it, and he was overwhelmed, saying, "My wife has wanted a blender like this! Thank you so much!" Only God could have arranged such divine connections.

In each place we visited, we were blessed to be a blessing—we were literally being pressed down with overwhelming abundance! At that point, we had to purchase two new suitcases because of the overflow of blessings we received! We ended that trip with six suitcases, filled to the maximum overweight capacity, and we were each holding multiple extra bags. This blessing was not a burden, but we certainly felt pressed down! The Spirit is teaching us how to receive such abundance—blessings unlike anything we have ever experienced in the past. Likewise, you will need to make room for the new overflow that God desires to bring into your life. Get ready for it!

LEVEL 4: "SHAKEN TOGETHER"

The next level of receiving is *"shaken together,"* which is even weightier. Your increased blessing is pressed down *and* shaken together.

Many years ago, when our son, Lincoln, was young, he came to me carrying a Lego catalog and said, "Daddy, I would like this one right here," and he pointed to one of the most expensive sets in the catalog. It cost approximately $500. Today, that is not the most expensive Lego set. Recently, I saw some that cost more than $1,000!

For us at the time, $500 was a lot of money. "Lincoln," I said, "if you really want that one, it's no problem, but you're going to have to believe God for it."

"Okay," he said, "I will." He told me he was going to start sowing his money, believing God for that Lego set. His faith was precious.

Not long after that, we went to Phoenix, Arizona, to minister at one of Patricia King's supernatural conferences. We would be there only one night and then catch a flight the next morning to Brisbane, Australia, for the beginning of a five-city Australian tour.

During the conference's offering that night, someone approached Lincoln and gave him a very nice gift—$50. It was not enough to buy the Lego set, but it was a large amount of money for a child. Lincoln looked at his mother and said, "I want to sow this money." She told him to go ahead, so he marched down to the front and placed the entire amount in the offering basket. That didn't seem to be the way to save for a Lego set, but Lincoln, in his childlike faith, was responding to the spiritual principle of sowing and reaping. If he could tap into the supernatural, he could have the toy his heart desired.

The great thing about it was that Lincoln didn't make a big deal of this or tell anyone what he was doing, and I didn't mention it from the pulpit. He just did it. He believed that God would provide the money for the Lego set, and he received it by faith.

The next day we embarked on our journey to Brisbane. No one in Australia knew anything about this desire of Lincoln's heart. No one knew what had happened in Phoenix and how he had responded. In Brisbane, as the offering was being received, before I went to the pulpit to preach, a man came up to Lincoln and handed him some Australian dollars (as I remember, it was about $200). No sooner had he handed the money to Lincoln than our son separated part of it and handed it to his mother. He said, "Mom, can you keep this for me? I'm going to take what I have here and give it in the offering."

The next city of our five-city tour was Sydney, and there Lincoln wanted to sow more of his money into the offering. After he did, someone came up to him and gave him more money. In the course of the services during the Australian tour, Lincoln, a mere child at the time, gave the equivalent of more than $2,000 in the offerings—and by the time we got to Perth, the last city on the tour, he already had enough money to buy the Lego set he wanted.

When Lincoln had first shown me the Lego catalog and told me what he wanted to buy, it was the month of May, and he had asked me, "How long do you think it will take me to get it?"

"Well, if you really trust God and believe in yourself, you could probably get it by Christmastime," I ventured.

Two weeks later, he already had what he needed to buy the Lego set. That set was the fruit of his seeding financial blessing in churches all over Australia, which became seeds in good soil and resulted in this harvest. On top of that, by sowing into ministry, Lincoln received the benefit of seeing souls won and deliverances and healings happen in Australia.

Our next stop after Australia was Hawaii, where I was to teach at the School of Signs and Wonders in Waikiki. Somehow, Lincoln learned that there was a Lego store in Honolulu and asked me to take him there. Not only was he able to buy the set he had so wanted, but he was also able to receive an abundance of additional Legos with some of the money he still had left.

The store had a new promotion in which customers could fill up a bucket of Legos for $14. It wasn't weighed. If something fit into the bucket, you could have it. Lincoln was learning about pressing down and shaking together, and believe me, he got his money's worth of Lego accessories. He and I spent more than an hour in that store figuring out how we could cram all the Lego items he wanted into that $14 bucket. God taught us a lot that day, and we received a compacted blessing. (I think they probably had to raise the price of the bucket after we left.)

Just as Lincoln was blessed by receiving the very generous offerings people gave him, and then reseeding those gifts to benefit others,

God wants you to be a generous receiver so you can then be an extraordinary, extravagant, and generous giver too.

LEVEL 5: "RUNNING OVER"

The fifth level of generous receiving in Luke 6:38 is *"running over."* God wants your blessing to be running over, *overflowing.* I love that word. There is an overflow of abundance in the realm of the Spirit.

LORD, I THANK YOU THAT YOU'RE NOT THE GOD OF JUST ENOUGH. YOU ARE THE LORD OF MORE, THE LORD OF THE OVERFLOW.

Some people say, "I have enough money to take care of my immediate bills. I have enough to take care of my daily life, enough to take care of myself"—but that's not good enough. The Lord of More—His proper name is El Shaddai—wants to move you into a place of extravagant blessing, a place of overflow where there is more than enough on every occasion so that you can become a generous giver, looking for opportunities to bless others. Wouldn't you love to become a person who blesses the nations of the earth? When a need arose, you could say, "Because God has blessed me, I am able to step in and meet that need."

Because our God supplies all our needs, we can concentrate on helping others. We aren't able to bless others in our own strength or abilities or because we happen to be financially prosperous. We are able to do this because we are children of God and citizens of heaven—people who are living in God's overflow. From that realm, blessing flows from our lives into the lives of others. Do you want to start living in overflow?

I have heard people say, "If I was blessed with a million dollars, I would definitely become more generous with my giving. I would be *very* generous. But right now I'm struggling. I have bills to pay, and I'm battling poverty." And there are a thousand other excuses that people use as a rationale for not being generous givers.

God established the tithe—giving 10 percent of our increase to Him—in Old Testament times. Today, there is much debate in the church as to whether or not believers are required to continue that principle in New Testament times. But think about it for a moment. Abraham gave a tithe of his goods to the priest Melchizedek, and this was before the institution of the law. (See Genesis 14:18–20.) In addition, ten percent is not extravagant or generous. We pay more than that in taxes. How much more should we honor the Lord with our wealth? Our financial gifts to His work are part of our praise and worship of Him. They honor Him. And when we honor God with our finances, what happens? It unlocks the door for us to come into the realms of heavenly abundance.

Regarding those who say they would be very generous if they had a million dollars, the truth is that they probably wouldn't give much more than they already are. If we can't learn to be generous with a little, we won't be generous with a lot. As I mentioned before, having money doesn't change a person; it only magnifies what's already in that person's heart. Those who are faithful with little will be faithful with much, and those who are not faithful with little will not be faithful with much.

Many people might not notice the offering of a widow who gave two mites, but Jesus did. (See, for example, Luke 21:1–3.) If a widow who was faithful in giving the little she had were to come into a large amount of money, the same Spirit of Generosity operating in her life would continue to work, and she would give according to the Spirit working in her—perhaps several hundred thousand dollars. Other people might then notice her generosity, although her offering would be the same proportion that she gave before she received abundance. In contrast, when people are stingy with the little they have, and they come into some money, it will be obvious to everyone how little they give and how very stingy they are.

God does not want His people to be stingy because He is not stingy. He so loved the world that He *gave*. That is the heart and nature of our God. He is the Spirit of Generosity. I thank God that Janet and I are operating in this revelation. It has changed our financial situation and our spiritual situation. It has changed every area of our lives.

When we live our lives poured out before the Lord, there is no limit to what we can give and receive. I have discovered that no matter how much I give to God—no matter how much I give of my emotions, or of my finances, or in sacrificing time away from my family for ministry purposes—He gives me back so much more. This is one of the keys we have put into practice in ministry, and it has kept our ministry going now for more than twenty years.

My wife and I have been blessed on several occasions to be invited to a traditional Louisiana crawfish boil while ministering with Pastors Kim and Vanessa Voisin at their great church, Vision Christian Center in Bourg. We've seen the crawfish being brought in—huge coolers full. We've seen the crawfish being washed and prepared while they were still alive. Then we've seen them go into the boiling pot along with potatoes, sausages, carrots, cauliflower, broccoli, corn on the cob, and large mushrooms. (It's making me hungry just thinking about it.)

What feasts these gatherings are, poured out for all to enjoy. After we eat for hours while reveling in good Christian fellowship, we enjoy King Cake and homemade beignets for a sweet dessert. The believers in Louisiana sure know how to enjoy life to the fullest! If we can experience such abundance in the natural, how much more supernatural overflow does God have available for us in every area of our lives? Much more!

GOD SO LOVED THE WORLD THAT HE *GAVE*.
THAT IS THE HEART AND NATURE OF OUR GOD.
HE IS THE SPIRIT OF GENEROSITY.

LEVEL 6: "POURED INTO YOUR LAP"

The sixth level of generous receiving is *"poured into your lap."* In the original context, this phrase refers to men and women showing great favor to you, bringing increase to your life in the places where you store your wealth. It speaks of spiritual and financial prosperity, as well as of divine favor, appointments, and connections. In this level, you move into a place of favor in the Spirit where you are blessed in unexpected ways from unexpected sources. Later you wonder, "How do I know that person? When did I meet them? Where did that special gift of favor come from? How did that door open?" There is often no way to explain how this level of generous receiving occurs—just expect it to happen more often.

Remember that each of these levels can open for you in ways that you expect, but the Spirit may also surprise you and introduce you to a new way of receiving His abundant blessings into your life! Janet and I enjoy going shopping because when you're led by the Spirit, it becomes a great adventure! You don't have to spend time and energy looking for sales. Instead, you can decree by the Spirit, "Sales are looking for me. God's favor is attracted to me!" When you do this, you will find "supernatural deals" and miracle connections everywhere you go!

Recently, while on a ministry trip, we stayed at a hotel that no longer provided comforters on the beds. This seemed very odd to us, and we weren't aware of the situation until it was late at night and we were getting into bed, only to discover there was merely a single sheet to cover us—in the middle of winter! The very next morning, I was determined to find appropriate bedding at a local store so we would be warm while we slept. I knew that God would give us what we needed, and that we would get it for an affordable price.

While we were in the bedding aisle, we found big, beautiful comforters that were regularly $80 each. We needed two, and the price tags were marked at a 50 percent discount. This seemed like a great deal, and I was thankful that the Lord had led us to find the comforters so quickly. However, even more amazing, when we checked out, the price rang up as $17 each. Wow! This sale came to us! This blessing was attracted to our lives! Abundance belongs to each and every child of God. Are you ready to receive it?

A woman named Sarah recently shared this testimony with us: "Last year in November, I unexpectedly had to receive a visitor for a few days. With no extra bed, I had to add a new sofa to my living room which would be comfortable for sleeping.... As I was listening to your teaching, you gave a testimony of how sales were looking for you. I suddenly felt I needed to pray in the Spirit and I declared that I would find good sales! I prayed and asked God to find the right sofa for me. Later, I went to the store and noticed a close-out sale and they had one week to move out. I got a great comfy sofa, at a very low price!"

We praise God for the divine connections He brings to His people. When you receive this revelation in your spirit, abundance will come looking for you; and when it does, you will recognize and welcome it!

Each of these levels can become a revelation to you. And as they do, you can point your faith with accuracy toward moving into the next level of increase in God.

LEVEL 7: "WITH THE MEASURE YOU USE, IT WILL BE MEASURED TO YOU"

There is one more level. Luke 6:38 says, *"For with the measure you use, it will be measured to you."* This is a great encouragement that tells us, "Don't stop! Don't give up! Keep going!"

Paul wrote to the Galatian believers, *"So let's not get tired of doing what is good. At just the right time ["in due season"* KJVER, NKJV] *we will reap a harvest of blessing if we don't give up"* (Galatians 6:9 NLT). Generously receive God's abundance—practice the art of being a grateful child who graciously receives from their generous Father. Generous believing produces generous receiving.

"At just the right time," or *"in due season,"* you will reap your harvest. That is…if you don't give up. You have every reason to remain faithful. An appointed harvest of abundance is coming. God has prepared a massive bounty just for you. The key is that you must continue moving in the things of God and allowing the things of God to move through you. You have no need to stockpile or hoard anything. Move forward in the Spirit—giving, receiving, releasing, receiving, and giving again. This is the way to enter into the abundance of God.

God is looking for people who will simply be generous receivers, people who will take Him at His Word and say to Him, "Lord, I will be a generous receiver of what You have for me. I will receive the abundance that flows from the open heavens. I will receive the unusual, the strange, the extraordinary miracles that You desire to release. Yes, God, I will receive them."

Let's pray together:

Heavenly Father, I thank You that You desire to pour out an extravagant, abundant blessing over Your people. I thank You for the vision You give us and for the favor You bestow on us to enable us to fulfill that vision. I thank You for the increase that comes from Your Spirit of Generosity, and I ask that You would give us a clearer understanding of how to partner with You in every level of becoming a generous receiver so we can move into new levels of being generous givers. In this way, Your generosity can flow and be manifested in our lives. In Jesus's mighty name, amen!

We are making great progress in unlocking all *7 Divine Mysteries*! The next mystery is sure to be a blessing as I share some wonderful angelic experiences God has given me, as well as personal stories from others who have tapped into angel power that makes abundance shower!

DECREES OF ABUNDANCE

As you decree and believe and receive the following truths, you can manifest unlimited abundance—now. Spirit, let it flow!

- *The power of God is working in me and supplying abundance on a daily basis.*

- *I receive the abundance of heavenly manna that is being supplied to me.*

- *I keep an attitude of gratitude so that an abundance of thanksgiving will continually flow through my thoughts.*

- *Whatever flows through me begins manifesting around me.*

- *God's abundant divine supply fills my spirit to overflowing.*

- *Abundance flows through me; therefore, abundance is manifesting around me.*

- *The windows of heaven are opened in my life to pour out overflowing abundance.*

CHAPTER 7

DIVINE MYSTERY #6: ANGEL POWER MAKES ABUNDANCE SHOWER

*"Bless the LORD, **you His angels, that excel in strength**, that do His commandments, hearkening to the voice of His word."*
—Psalm 103:20

One of the supernatural signs that often accompanies my ministry is an awareness of angelic movement. Those who are present at my meetings often report seeing, sensing, feeling, or hearing angels in the room as I preach the Word. In February 2020, when I was ministering at a session during the Winter Campmeeting in Ashland, Virginia, I suddenly sensed a swift shift in the atmosphere. The present-day reality of angels was being confirmed to me once again. Through my spirit, I could see angels of abundance coming into the meeting and releasing an impartation to those who were present and willing to receive it. Moments earlier, I had been speaking about the ministry of angels described throughout Scripture, along with God's promises of abundant life—but now, this reality was manifesting in the room for me to witness firsthand. Such manifestations should not surprise us. After all, the Bible says, *"The disciples went everywhere and preached, and*

the Lord worked through them, confirming what they said by many miracu-
lous signs" (Mark 16:20 NLT).

The two angels who manifested at the Ashland meeting appeared to be just slightly larger than the size of an average person. Their faces shone with the glory of the Lord, and their wings were filled with brilliant light. They wore glistening robes with intricate golden details embroidered all around the collars. But what struck me most about these angels was that their arms were filled to overflowing with fruit of all kinds. There were oranges, apples, grapes, bananas, peaches… it was like a cornucopia of abundance. Later, when I told my friend Debbie Kendrick what I had seen that night, she said, "Those were angels of fruitfulness." Instantly, I received a confirmation in my spirit of her Spirit-quickened revelation. I would experience increased fruitfulness in the days ahead because God had assigned these angels to my life.

When I saw those angels in the meeting, I had a strong sense that God was equipping us for the coming days. To me, those two angels appearing in such a marvelous way spoke of "double blessings" and an "abundance of good things." I didn't realize at the time that the world was about to change in a very drastic way. This meeting was the very last service that I preached in before the coronavirus pandemic began to shut down everything in America. As an itinerant minister, my entire schedule was almost instantly cancelled, but I still had hope—for God's angels were working in my life to help realign our ministry with a new focus.

I thank God for His insights and divine visions that give us great hope. In the following days, I had a strong sense of the Spirit's abiding presence surrounding us and giving us His peace. Little by little, as Janet and I sensitively followed the guidance of the Lord, we found ourselves doing things we had never done before. The Spirit led us to begin our weekly *Glory Bible Study* online, where we could teach, train, and equip believers worldwide with supernatural truths. Over the past year, our ministry has flourished, and we are reaching more people than ever before. Each week, the lost are being saved, the sick are being healed, and the spiritually hungry are being filled with God's glory—so much fruitfulness! You see, we may not always understand the reasons why God assigns His angels to our lives, but if we are open to His flow, we can enter into a place of divine encounter and abundant provision.

GOD'S MESSENGERS

I understand that many fine believers are filled with fear when it comes to encountering angels. A number of them fear anything supernatural. However, when we enter the divine supernatural realm, we access God's glory. In His glory, there is safety and nothing to fear. We enter His glory realm through the blood of Jesus and through the safety of His Word.

I also understand that many people are wary of dealing with angels because they are unsure about their origin, wondering how to know if they are truly from God and not a demonic manifestation. But what I share with you in this chapter about God's angels and their role in our receiving abundance is scriptural. It will *not* connect you with any demons.

Whenever God's angels speak to you, it is as if the very voice of God is speaking. His angels do not speak on their own accord or of their own desire. They don't just say what they choose to say. When messenger angels come, they bring a godly message directly from heaven. That is why, if the words you hear an angel say do not line up with the Word of God, you will know instantly that particular angel is not from God. Every angel sent to you from God will speak a message that falls directly in line with His Word and His will for your life. Knowing this will protect you and keep you from being deceived.

According to the Bible, we don't praise angels, we don't worship angels, and we don't pray to angels. Angels are never to be put on a pedestal, for they are not God. They are God's servants and our servants. But I thank God for the angels because they have very specific and important roles to play in the life of every believer. This includes enabling us to receive financial blessings.

ANGELS OF ABUNDANCE

It is my personal belief that along with every promise God has given us, He has also assigned a group of angels over that promise

to help bring it to pass. Hebrews 1:14 says that *"angels are only ser-*
vants—spirits sent to care for people who will inherit salvation" (NLT).
Angels are God's servants assigned to your life to see that His purposes—abundance in every area—are fulfilled in you. This is part of
the promise of Deuteronomy 8:18, which we discussed earlier in this
book.

There are many different ways to connect to God's angels.[18] We can
see angels at work in the Scriptures, and we can also experience them
today. We can sense them, see them, hear them, or feel their presence
in the atmosphere.

There is an entire class of angels known as angels of abundance.
These angels take on various tasks, and they go by many different
names. There are angels of blessing, angels of provision, angels of
finance and favor, and angels of prosperity. Even though they go by
different names, they all work together in this arena to accomplish
God's purposes through His people.

The Bible speaks of angels as harvesters. (See Matthew 13:39.) So,
when you are involved in sowing and reaping for the kingdom, you
have to get the angels involved. They will help you harvest the fruits
of seeds you have planted. Perhaps you planted seed in another place,
and then you moved. Send the angels to bring back that harvest. If
you have moved on in God, gone forward in Him, an angel will know
where that seed was sown and can bring back a harvest from distant
fields where you scattered seed.

Angels of blessing are connected to Proverbs 10:22, which says,
"The blessing of the Lord makes one rich, and He adds no sorrow with it"
(NKJV). This is not just any blessing. It is the blessing of the Lord, and
His angels are connected to His blessing. When angels of abundance
show up in your life, get ready for the riches of God to overtake you.
These angels come with unlimited blessings, the kind of blessings that
flow from the very presence of Jesus: *"My God shall supply all your need*
according to His riches in glory by Christ Jesus" (Philippians 4:19 NKJV).

Do you realize that you can ask for angelic assistance in the area
of abundance? When we are living in Christ and Christ is living in us,
we can use our believer's authority to invite these angels to show up

---

18. For more teaching on angels and new realms of abundance, see my book *Seeing Angels*.

and pour out heavenly riches in our lives—whether we see the angels or not. The important thing is that you recognize the blessing, and the best part is that you don't have to worry about this kind of blessing bringing with it any devastation or sorrow. After some people get rich, their lives quickly fall apart. That's because they don't know how to handle money, and money starts handling them. Money can be a terrible taskmaster. But when the angels of abundance show up, they come in partnership with angels of wisdom.

When you speak about the realities of God, those realities come into your midst. When you begin to give testimony to what God has done and what He is doing, that testimony opens the door to more of His glory. In that moment, angels of blessing and angels of wisdom can appear and begin to work in combination in your life. Again, when you receive His abundance, His wisdom and blessing come too. You get wisdom with your blessings so that you know how to steward them properly. And, of course, God receives all the glory because of it.

WHEN THE ANGELS OF ABUNDANCE SHOW UP, THEY COME IN PARTNERSHIP WITH ANGELS OF WISDOM.

If you want to experience this abundance, just lift your spirit up to Him and receive:

Father, in the name of Jesus, I thank You for sending Your angels of abundance, including Your angels of blessing and Your angels of wisdom. We invite these angels to work in cooperation in our lives even now. In Jesus's mighty name, amen!

Angels of wisdom will speak truth to you or nudge you in a godly direction. They will bring you insight and knowledge regarding your finances. Far too many people live in fear and anxiety over their financial state. The word *mortgage* literally means "dead pledge,"[19] and many people who have a mortgage on their home feel that they are in a death grip. Maybe we need to make a practice of calling a mortgage a "home

---

19. Lexico.com, Oxford University Press, © 2021, https://www.lexico.com/definition/mortgage.

loan." That's all it is. It is not a death pledge or a death grip, and it will not take you to the grave. The Spirit is making a way for you to get through it! When you move into the realm of manifesting abundance, you'll have more than enough finances to pay off your home and live debt-free. It's God's desire for you to live free from debt. (See Romans 13:8.) When you get the angels moving in this way, your entire financial outlook will change.

One time, when I was preaching in the bayous of Louisiana, I taught about God's angels and their connection to our finances. A woman came up to me after the meeting and said that when she was a child, her father was a serious gambler. When he received his weekly paycheck on Friday night, he would take it directly to a casino. Very often, he didn't come home until Sunday evening. By then, of course, he had lost the majority of his pay.

The woman often overheard her parents quarreling over groceries and other family needs because their money never quite went far enough. She remembered times when there was nothing but crackers in the house to tide them over, and she was often hungry. Her poor mother was under the constant pressure of the knowledge that her husband was wasting away his hard-earned paycheck, and of not having enough money to properly care for her children. The children had to live in that atmosphere of lack and the fear it created.

This woman said that as I was teaching, the Spirit of God revealed to her that she was suffering from a fear of financial lack and that it was tied to that early childhood trauma. Was that knowledge enough for her to overcome her fear? Not fully, but knowing is half the battle.

When God begins to shine the light of His revelation upon you, and angels of wisdom come and begin to show you areas in your life where the enemy has tried to gain access, where he has attempted to take hold of your affairs, God is up to something good. He will deliver you from those limitations and bring you forth into the blessing of His glorious light. He gives you revelation so you can deal with any situation by submitting that part of your life, your heart, your past, to Him, and watching Him do a miracle.

The woman instantly confessed the sin of fear over her finances that had held her captive. She gave it all to God and was totally set free.

I wrote down her precise words: "I am no longer afraid to be obedient to God regarding finances."

And you, too, can be free from whatever has hindered your abundance. Whatever it is, God wants to deliver you right now. You are God's child, and His will is for you to prosper in every way.

HAVING CHILDLIKE FAITH TO BELIEVE

As a young child, I often saw angels. Initially, I didn't know they were angels because it was so common for me to see them on a daily basis. I even played with them in our backyard. When I rode on the swings, the angels and I would sing together. My mom would hear me singing whenever I went outside. Sometimes even the next door neighbor could hear me. He even commented to my mother, "You know, Joshua was singing very loudly today in the backyard."

When I would tell my parents about being in the backyard with my friends, they would call them my "imaginary friends" because they couldn't see who I was talking about. May I propose to you that there are many things in the Spirit that you can't see, but that doesn't mean they are "imaginary"? It just means that you haven't unlocked that door with revelation—yet.

Let's start unlocking some of those doors. Healing is available for you. Hope is with you right now. There is an abundance of provision all around you. According to Philippians 4:19, you are surrounded by God's *"riches in glory by Christ Jesus."* As a believer, you are an heir of salvation with access to the wealth of heaven. God's glory envelops your life right now. If you can capture this revelation in the Spirit, you can grab hold of it and pull it down. If you don't see it, you might just let it pass by you.

Several years ago, I ministered at a conference hosted by our friends Russ and Mave Moyer. I was staying in a hotel in Oakville, Ontario, near Toronto. One afternoon, I was walking from the bedroom to the bathroom when I suddenly seemed to step into a wind tunnel, and, in the Spirit, I saw money flying all around me. It was above me and below me and on either side of me. All I had to do was take hold of it. That experience changed my perception. I suddenly realized that I didn't have to pray, "God, please bring Your provision." It was right there. I just needed to reach out and receive it.

ABUNDANCE IS ALL AROUND YOU— REACH OUT AND RECEIVE IT.

Again, there are many things in the Spirit that we have not yet seen, but that doesn't mean they're not real. We just haven't recognized them. Most believers are missing a lot of what is available to them because they are not perceiving it in the Spirit. Instead of begging God for money to meet our needs, we should pray, "God, open the eyes of my heart. Bring me Your revelation. Give me Your wisdom in mind and spirit. Let me see the things You have available for me. Thank You for it even now."

One of the unseen realities that I have discussed throughout this book is the presence of angels in our lives. As I said, when I was a child, I used to see angels in my backyard, but I also saw them at church. I saw angels gliding around the church sanctuary. I sat with a friend named Sara, and she saw them too. To us, the ceiling of that church seemed so very high, and angels were up there flying back and forth in worship. We never tired of watching them.

One of the amazing things about those angels is that I don't remember seeing any wings on them, and yet they had no problem flying around. I have seen angels with huge wings, and they seem to be standing still. Others, who have no visible wings, float through the air. The glory is always an interesting realm!

One Sunday, Sara and I were at the back of the sanctuary talking about seeing the angels, and a group of adults overheard us. One man decided he needed to correct us. "You can't see angels," he said. "Nobody can see angels." He got quite upset with us. I tried to explain what I was seeing, and Sara did too, but he would have none of it. "Stop telling stories!" he insisted. "You're making up lies!"

Well, adults were supposed to know better than children. They had lived much longer and had more experience than youngsters. Adults have wisdom, and we were taught to respect them, so this rebuke had a profound effect on us. I caution present-day elders of the church to be careful when instructing children. You must guard the childlike faith of the younger generations because the Bible says that *"death and life are in the power of the tongue"* (Proverbs 18:21). What we say can unlock things in the Spirit world, but what we say can also bind and shut things in the Spirit world, depending on the content of our words. It is important to bind the work of the enemy, but please don't bind the things of God just because you don't understand them.

The words spoken over us that day had an adverse effect on my spiritual life. I didn't want to be considered a liar. So, for me, the angelic realm was closed. For years to come, I was no longer aware of the presence of angels. Looking back, I believe they were still there; I simply didn't know it. They didn't leave; I just didn't see them anymore. My eyes were shut to their presence.

I thank God that He has spiritual eye salve to use on us. He can put this healing balm on our blinded eyes and cause them to see again. Paul prayed,

> *That the God of our Lord Jesus Christ, the Father of glory, may give to you the spirit of wisdom and revelation in the knowledge of Him:* **the eyes of your understanding being enlightened***; that you may know what is the hope of His calling, and what* **the riches of the glory of His inheritance** *in the saints, and what is the exceeding greatness of His power to us-ward who believe, according to the working of His mighty power.* (Ephesians 1:17–19)

You may be seeing some things in the Spirit realm, but God wants to show you more. It was not the eyes of our head that Paul prayed for; it was the eyes of our understanding. If you are physically blind, then, yes, God wants to open those eyes. Yet, too many of us see well with our physical eyes but see poorly with the eyes of our understanding. Let Him open the eyes of your heart to see more spiritual realities. Let's pray about that together right now:

> Father, in the name of Jesus, I ask You to open the eyes of my heart to see what is going on around me. I want to see into Your glory realm and know what You have made available to

me so that I can lay hold of it. God, I want to see with revelation, with understanding, with wisdom, the mysteries of Your glory. I let go of everything that has tried to bind me and blind me in the realm of the Spirit. Lord, renew my childlike faith today to connect with You in a brand-new way. In Jesus's mighty name, amen!

There are many ways God can reopen the realm of childlike faith for us, many different ways He can allow us to see with the eyes of our heart into the realms of His glory. One of those ways is through our dreams, and those dreams can involve angels. Far too many people are willing to discount their dreams. "That's not real," they say. "That's not valid or legitimate." Well, not every dream is a spiritual dream, but God wants to give you spiritual dreams. And, when He gives you those spiritual dreams, He wants you to pay attention to what He's showing you through them. For me, such dreams are so vivid, so real, and so living that they seem much more like encounters than dreams. These encounters are more than a prophetic insight, and they are not just God speaking through images. It is as though I'm in an actual encounter, face-to-face with the angels that God has placed in my life. When this happens, there's an understanding, a revelation that I capture in that moment, and I am able to grab hold of what God is saying and what He's doing through His angels.

Genesis 28 tells of a dream Jacob had that was more than a mere dream. He was traveling and stopped for the night. He laid his head on a rock for a pillow and went to sleep. Remember, Jesus is the Rock— He is the foundation for every spiritual encounter. So when we set our minds on Jesus, placing our heads on the Rock, He moves on our behalf.

That night, Jacob had a wonderful dream. He saw a ladder extending between heaven and earth, and he saw angels going up and down that ladder. This is an important revelation about angels. They don't just stay in heaven and come to earth every once in a while. They are constantly going back and forth, bringing God's favor to His people. There are many angels in heaven—we could never count them all— but there are also many angels here on earth. In fact, there may be more here than there.

Psalm 91 guarantees us that each believer has at least two angels. I have at least two, and you have at least two. Why do I say that? Psalm 91:11 says, *"He shall give His **angels** charge over you...."* The word "angel" is plural—*"angels"* means more than one angel.

Jacob saw a lot more than two angels. They were going up and down from earth to heaven and back to earth again. Let's read this important passage of Scripture:

> *And he dreamed, and behold a ladder set up on the earth, and the top of it reached to heaven: and behold the **angels of God ascending and descending** on it. And, behold, the LORD stood above it, and said, I am the LORD God of Abraham your father, and the God of Isaac: the land whereon you lie, to you will I give it, and to your seed; and your seed shall be as the dust of the earth, and you shall spread abroad to the west, and to the east, and to the north, and to the south: and in you and in your seed shall all the families of the earth be blessed. And, behold, I am with you, and will keep you in all places wherever you go, and will bring you again into this land; for I will not leave you, until I have done that which I have spoken to you of. And Jacob awakened out of his sleep, and he said, Surely the LORD is in this place; and I knew it not. And he was afraid, and said, How dreadful [awesome] is this place! this is no other but the house of God, and this is the gate of heaven.* (Genesis 28:12–17)

The Lord was standing above the heavenly ladder, and He confirmed His promises to Jacob: he and his descendants were to be blessed. When Jacob woke up, he remembered the dream. He remembered the ladder, he remembered the angels, and he remembered the voice of God from above it all. It was very real, and he knew that it was a dream from God. Then Jacob did something very important. He made a vow to God:

> *And Jacob vowed a vow, saying, If God will be with me, and will keep me in this way that I go, and will give me bread to eat, and raiment to put on, so that I come again to my father's house in peace; then shall the LORD be my God: and this stone, which I have set for a pillar, shall be God's house: and of all that You shall give me I will surely give the tenth to You.* (Genesis 28:20–22)

When God speaks, angels get moving. They carry out His words. But we have to get moving too. The angels were moving, and Jacob could see them moving. They were going up to heaven and bringing down what God had promised and releasing it to Jacob. They were doing their part. An impartation was coming to Jacob's life. Now Jacob had to do his part. He knew this was real, so he had to respond. What God had promised was a great inheritance, a great generational blessing, and Jacob could not afford to miss it.

"Surely the LORD is in this place," Jacob said. This was much more than a dream. When the reality of it all finally struck Jacob, he was suddenly frightened. It was such an awe-inspiring experience. Imagine waking up from such a spiritual encounter and feeling fear. But that's a supernatural secret that should tell us something.

"Religious" spirits would immediately say that this dream wasn't from God; otherwise, Jacob wouldn't have felt any fear. But we must use spiritual discernment. Don't throw something wonderful away because you don't understand it. Some things that come from God engender fear. Many men and women of God in the Bible felt fear upon seeing angels, and you might too.

Going somewhere totally new is sometimes frightening. Seeing something you have never seen before is sometimes frightening. Our human tendency is to be afraid of anything we have not encountered before. But we can get over it. God has promised us so many blessings. I feel confident that you can handle it. Get over all your fears by trusting that God has your back.

"Don't be afraid," angels say when they come as messengers and helpers to people. (See, for example, Luke 1:30; 2:10.) How tragic it would be to miss a blessing because we were frightened by how that blessing came to us. As I wrote earlier, too many believers are afraid that the angel they see may be a demon. Believe me, if you love God and are grounded in His Word, you will know the difference. Our natural tendency is to be afraid of new things, but God wants to take us into new spiritual territory.

Jacob said, *"How dreadful* [awesome] *is this place! this is no other but the house of God, and this is the gate of heaven."* A gateway, a doorway, a portal into the heavenlies had opened, and it had come to Jacob through a dream. Let's start dreaming big...and then even bigger.

THE GLORY OF GOD'S PRESENCE

Sadly, because someone injected an element of doubt and fear into my young mind about the reality of angels, I went the rest of my childhood without seeing these servants of God, His messengers. I spent my teenage years without the benefit of recognizing angels and the strength they provide. I loved the Lord and wanted to live for Him and serve Him—but I didn't see angels. The words that person had spoken over my life so many years earlier had blocked my spiritual eyes from discerning them. I needed to break free from that bondage, and the Lord brought me release as I worshipped Him and learned more about Him so that I could be ready to receive the revelation and supernatural manifestations He would send to me.

I went to church every time the church doors were open. I even started attending special meetings. Besides Sunday worship services, I went to midweek prayer meetings and Friday night Bible studies. I was hungry for more of God and wanted to be where He was moving.

There is something to be said for "soaking in the Spirit," which refers to spending a long period of time worshipping in God's presence and receiving His healing, wisdom, and strength. When we soak in the Spirit, He ministers to us layer by layer, dealing with those things that the enemy spirit has put on us. Like peeling away the layers of an onion, God peels away the deceit and wrong teachings we have accepted. The deeper you go in the Spirit, the more ungodly layers come off.

When soaking, you may be touched by the Spirit and begin to weep; and as you weep in God's presence, the more power you feel working in you. God could do this restoration all at once, but He wants to test your faithfulness, so He usually does it over time. As you continue to rest in His presence, He is working in your spirit to rid you of every hindrance so you can take wing and fly. When the glory of God is present, you can bring all your problems and worries and leave them there. You can lay everything you're currently going through at the feet of Jesus, and then begin to dance for joy because you're free. You can be changed in His manifest presence—the glory!

In my early twenties, I preached at the campground in Ashland, Virginia. While I was there, as I slept, I had a very strange encounter. Since it happened at night while I was sleeping, we could say it was a dream, but it felt more like a very real encounter.

In my encounter, three men walked out of a cloud toward me. The strange thing was that all three looked like me, although a bit broader in the shoulders and a little taller. They could have been my older brothers. They introduced themselves, telling me their names and their ministry purpose. Very quickly, I understood that they were three angels assigned to my life by God. Although they had been with me my whole life, I hadn't known it until then.

Why did this spiritual breakthrough happen at that point in my life and not earlier? I think that by then, after the times I had spent in God's presence, I had finally stopped believing the lie that I couldn't see angels. As a result, I was reconnected to the angelic realm through a dream. That night, a lot of spiritual dots were connected for me, and things began to fall into place. The same thing might happen for you through a vision or some other way. The important thing is to bask in God's presence as much as you can— do it with an open mind, an open spirit, and a genuine hunger for something more from Him.

There was more to my dream, but when I woke up from that encounter, I was determined to pursue God in this new realm. I didn't want to miss what He had available for me. I was determined to research all the Scriptures that had anything to do with angels.

I did some serious searching through the Bible, looking up everything under the words *angel, angels, angelic, cherub, cherubim, seraph, seraphim, angelic hosts, holy ones,* and more. I noticed that there were 394 individual Scriptures that had something to say about the realm of the angels, which to me meant it clearly was an important subject.[20]

---

20. I have included this list of Scriptures in my book *Seeing Angels,* Appendix II, "Angels in the Bible—394 Scripture References."

Some ministers may preach for months on topics the Bible has very little to say about, sometimes only a few verses, without anyone objecting. And yet, when I started preaching about angels, I discovered that people with religious spirits got very riled up. Why was that? Because nothing threatens the enemy more than when believers realize they have authority over the angelic realm.

Furthermore, when the enemy is revealed or exposed for who he is, he goes ballistic. Believers must understand that Satan is not the opposite of God. Satan was once equivalent to archangels such as Michael or Gabriel—but there is no way he should ever be compared to God. Satan is a created being, and God is the Creator. God has no equal. None. He is sitting upon His throne, high and lifted up, and His glory is filling the heavenly temple. (See Isaiah 6:1.) Additionally, the name of Jesus is higher than the name of any and every angel that can be named. Jesus's name is higher than anyone or anything. (See Philippians 2:9–11.) And where does Jesus live? He lives inside you and me, and He gives us His power and authority. When you understand the believer's authority, the whole realm of angels is suddenly no longer intimidating. As a believer in Jesus Christ, you have authority in the spiritual realm. Period.

This authority extends to power over the demonic realm. Jesus was very clear on this subject when He said, *"They will cast out demons"* (Mark 16:17 NKJV, AMP, NLT). Who will cast out demons? Believers. We can cast them out. They are under our feet, and we have authority over them. We do not have to fear fallen, demonic angels, and we do not have to fear God's good angels. Why is it, then, that so many believers are afraid of angels? Jesus Christ, the Hope of Glory, is living inside you. What do you have to fear? He wants to manifest His authority and power in the spiritual realm and on earth through your words and your actions.

THROUGH JESUS CHRIST, YOU HAVE AUTHORITY IN THE SPIRITUAL REALM.

GLORY AND ANGELS

Isaiah 6 answers some of the questions most believers have about angels, their proper place, their proper order, and how angels interact with the work of the Holy Spirit in and through us. Isaiah had a prophetic vision in which he saw angels at work:

> In the year that king Uzziah died I saw also the LORD sitting upon a throne, high and lifted up, and His train filled the temple. **Above it stood the seraphims:** each one had six wings; with two he covered his face, and with two he covered his feet, and with two he did fly. And one cried to another, and said, Holy, holy, holy, is the LORD of hosts: the whole earth is full of His glory. And the posts of the door moved at the voice of him that cried, and the house was filled with smoke. Then said I, Woe is me! for I am undone; because I am a man of unclean lips, and I dwell in the midst of a people of unclean lips: for my eyes have seen the King, the LORD of hosts. **Then flew one of the seraphims to me,** having a live coal in his hand, which he had taken with the tongs from off the altar: and he laid it upon my mouth, and said, Lo, this has touched your lips; and your iniquity is taken away, and your sin purged. Also I heard the voice of the Lord, saying, Whom shall I send, and who will go for Us? Then said I, Here am I; send me. And He said, Go, and tell this people, Hear you indeed, but understand not; and see you indeed, but perceive not. (Isaiah 6:1–9)

Some people want to have a theological discussion about whether or not seraphim are angels and whether angels can be seraphim. We could go in a million different directions and never resolve the issue. But something we can all agree on is that seraphim are heavenly beings. To my way of thinking, with our knowledge from the Word of God about what angels are and how they operate, seraphims fall into that classification. The word *seraphim* means "burning."[21] Angels that are bright and shining, full of fire and light, fit that description as seraphim.

The seraphim had wings they used to cover their faces and feet and also to fly. These heavenly creatures of brilliant, burning light cried out to one another, saying, "Holy, holy, holy, is the LORD of hosts."

---

21. *Strong's*, #H8314.

Notice that they called Him *"the LORD of hosts,"* meaning the Lord over the angel armies. *"The whole earth is full of His glory,"* they concluded.

These angels were doing two things: (1) revealing themselves in Isaiah's presence and (2) giving glory to the Lord. The angels of God never bring glory to themselves. They don't show up just so we will say how wonderful they are. They show up so that we will say, "How wonderful Jesus is! How wonderful our Lord is! He alone is worthy of all glory, honor, and praise." The angels know this, so they worship God. In this case, they called Him *"the King, the LORD of hosts."* This is one of His names.

If you desire to see angels at work, begin targeting that goal in your prayers by recognizing the Lord of angelic hosts at work in your life. Give God the place of prominence. Put Him in that position, and then yield to His authority so He can dispatch the hosts of heaven to work on your behalf.

When the seraphim declared, *"The whole earth is full of His glory,"* the doorposts of the temple suddenly began shaking, and the house filled with smoke. Giving God the praise He deserves brings a shaking. Where His glory is, there are angels; and where angels are, there you will find His glory. Glory and angels go together. They carry the glory, and they usher in the glory wherever they go.

When all of this transpired, something happened to Isaiah. He suddenly declared, *"Woe is me! for I am undone; because I am a man of unclean lips, and I dwell in the midst of a people of unclean lips: for my eyes have seen the King, the LORD of hosts."* Every time the glory of God manifests, it changes us. We can never leave the glory the same way we came. As we worship with the angels, declaring, "Only You are worthy, only You deserve the glory," in that place of humbling ourselves before the greatness of who God is, a new impartation comes to us.

Next, one of the seraphim flew to do his job. He took a hot coal from off the altar and approached Isaiah to cleanse his lips. And the angel spoke. What did he say? *"Lo, this has touched your lips; and your iniquity is taken away, and your sin purged."* The angel was not imparting his word but rather God's word.

Then Isaiah heard the audible voice of the Lord saying, *"Whom shall I send, and who will go for Us?"* Isaiah, moved and prepared by what he was experiencing, answered, *"Here am I; send me."* This response was remarkable because he suddenly went from saying how undone and unworthy he was to receiving personal ministry and then being ready for his call. He was responding to the Lord of Hosts.

The Lord of Hosts was issuing a call, but who would carry out that call? Who would carry out that ministry function? It wasn't God who flew to the altar and picked up a hot coal to purge Isaiah. It wasn't God who then flew to Isaiah's side and placed that coal upon his lips. This was the work of the angel. Under God's direction, the angel provided strength for Isaiah to stand up and fulfill his calling.

So, can we be ministered to by an angel? Can we communicate with angels? If we read the Scriptures carefully, there can be no doubt about this. God has ordained His heavenly hosts to perform many functions on His behalf, and many of those functions are for our benefit. God is God, and He is King. In the natural, it would not be correct for a king to get up from his throne and carry out his own decrees. After all, he's the king. He doesn't have to do that. He has his subjects, his servants, to carry out his will. It is the same way in the spiritual realm. God assigns His angels to carry out His will—and they aid God's children to do the same.

Angels do God's bidding. They are His faithful hosts. When they speak, they are not speaking on their own authority. They only speak when God tells them to speak, and they only say what He tells them to say. In the same way, when angels act, they are not acting on their own behalf or on their own authority. They are only doing what the Lord of Hosts commands them to do, nothing more and nothing less.

The voice of an angel, therefore, is an extension of God's voice; and the hand of an angel is an extension of God's hand. God could have done it all Himself. He knows how to grasp tongs and take a hot coal from an altar. He knows how to place a burning coal on a person's lips to purge them. He knows what to say and how to say it. But again, why should He do it all? He is God. He is King. He is the Lord of heaven's angelic hosts.

Thank God we have a role in this process too. Jesus sits on the throne of our hearts, and He allows us to take part in the affairs of His kingdom. He assigns us the work, empowers us to do it, and provides for our every need as we carry it out. When we need help, the hosts of heaven stand at the ready to come to our rescue, to give us strength for the task. They attend to the orders of the King.

We can take this a step further. As we have seen, the Scriptures declare that God has made *us* to be kings and priests unto Him. That's why God has assigned angels to be with us, to protect us, to attend to our needs, and to help us with our heavenly assignments.

Some people think that angels could perhaps appear once in a while, but I'm telling you that they are present with you every hour of every day, and they respond to the words coming from your mouth. When you speak with the authority of God, who is inside you and rules and reigns on the throne of your heart, angels rush to bring to pass what you have declared.

GOD HAS ASSIGNED ANGELS TO BE WITH YOU, TO PROTECT YOU, TO ATTEND TO YOUR NEEDS, AND TO HELP YOU WITH YOUR HEAVENLY ASSIGNMENTS.

That's why the major assignment of the enemy is to get you to doubt God's Word. If you doubt His Word, you won't speak it; and if you doubt His Word, you won't see it come to pass. If you are uncertain about God's Word, you won't move into it. If you don't believe and speak the Word, your angels are frustrated, standing idle, with nothing to act on. Remember, they have no personal agenda. They work to fulfill the purposes of God, nothing else, and they are waiting for you to speak His will.

God is looking for people in this day who know their God, know their authority as believers, and know how to loose angels of abundance. Are you one of those people? Let's pray together to yield to His purposes:

Lord, I thank You that Your glory is with us and that Your glory is flowing. Thank You that Your glory is bringing us divine revelation. Now we can see You in ways we have not seen You before. Now we can know You in ways we have not known You before. We long to cooperate with heaven in a new way. In every moment, may there be a yielding of our spirits, souls, and physical bodies to the purposes of Your glory! God, may Your Word, Your truth, flow through us so that we will have more boldness. As we proclaim that Word, we know that our angels of abundance will be assigned to bring to fulfillment the words we speak. Amen!

When you speak the Word of God, it creates a highway in the Spirit realm, a direct link angels can travel on to carry out God's purposes here on earth. If you speak out the Word, you will see angels activated in your home. Speak out the Word over your finances, and angels of abundance will appear, bringing a flow of funds and blessings into your life. Speak the Word over your physical body, and you will see healing miracles come to you through the intervention of God's heavenly hosts, His angels.[22]

Too often, we feel all alone, but the truth is that we are surrounded by a heavenly host, a mass gathering. Even now, it is hovering over and around you. Feel the protection of God's faithful angelic servants guarding your life, watching over you continually. If you can't see them working in the situations and circumstances of your daily life, know that they are nevertheless present, and the presence of God's angels of abundance is increasing in this day of His glory. His abundant glory has made the way. We can now walk in that glory, participate in that glory, and see that glory overtaking us in every area of life.

ANGELS CLEAR THE WAY

*He said to me, "**The LORD**, before whom I walk, **will send His angel with you** and prosper your way."* (Genesis 24:40 NKJV)

In this verse, Abraham is speaking instructions to his servant Eliezer. He is preparing to send Eliezer to go find a wife fit for his son Isaac. It was time for Isaac to wed, and Abraham needed just the right

---

22. I designed my perpetual desktop calendar *Activating Angels 365* to enable people to easily speak God's prophetic Word over their lives on a daily basis.

woman for him, for Isaac was heir to the promises of God. He could not marry just anyone. He needed the right spouse.

Abraham was very clear when instructing his servant. An angel, he said, would go before him and prosper his way. And what was his mission? To find a suitable wife for Isaac. God would send His angel to help Eliezer successfully fulfill this important mission. This tells me that finding the proper spouse, the right person, a godly spouse, a supernatural helper or helpmeet, is actually a form of prosperity in your life.

The richest treasures I have in the natural are my wife and my children. My wife is more precious to me than gold, silver, diamonds, or any other natural thing. She is an absolute gem. It has been said, "Behind every man of God, there is a mighty woman of God." That is true for me. Janet is absolutely amazing, and I hope she knows how much I love her.

God assigned an angel to Eliezer's mission to make it successful. Likewise, specific angels have also been assigned to you to make your ways successful. Not only do you have angels assigned to you, but those angels faithfully accompany you everywhere you go to give you strength, to keep you safe, and to prosper your way. If you pay attention to the reality of these prosperity angels being assigned to you, it will change the way you think and speak.

Not long ago, I was telling someone on the phone about some very big and unusual dreams God had put in my spirit. The person asked me, "Well, where are you going to get the money for that?"

I said, "Do you realize angels of prosperity work with me?"

We are not led by fear or intimidation. We're not led by how much or how little we have in our pockets or in the bank. We are not led by our good credit rating or lack of it. We are led forth by God, knowing that angels of abundance have been assigned to our lives, and they go ahead of us and clear the way.

If we follow the Holy Spirit, we can be sure that, as we speak God's Word, we are activating those angels, and God will watch over His Word to ensure that it manifests in our lives. When we are accompanied by angels of abundance, we can be certain of the outcome.

We received an exciting testimony from Robert in North Carolina who had an awesome testimony about angels of abundance working in his life: "Sleeping on a friend's couch, all my possessions in a couple of bags, I had been brought to naught. Zero. Nothing. Early one morning just before waking, I had a dream. In the dream I was on the very same couch with two angels standing next to me in drab brown, burlap robes. One leaned over with an "Angel Money Pillow" to slip under my head. What does this pillow look like? It seemed to be a one-quart plastic bag filled with neatly stacked and banded one hundred dollar bills. I awakened immediately to find no one standing there, yet I sensed a very real heavenly presence. I rejoiced in knowing that my breakthrough was very close at hand. Almost exactly one month later, through God's grace, I miraculously received $17,100.13! Praise God, He brought me up out of a horrible pit!"

God has angels that work in mysterious ways—and we must welcome their ministry in our lives. When we do, we will walk in new realms of divine abundance.

At the beginning of the coronavirus crisis in the United States, we heard about the empty store shelves. Many people were having difficulty finding the items they needed. However, we had first heard about the toilet paper shortage from friends in Australia. They told us there was none to be found and that we had better stock up because the shortage was coming to North America too. Fortunately, we got a head start on getting supplies of toilet paper and had such a good stock that we were able to help other people when they could find none.

One evening, Janet asked me to go to the grocery store, and she made me a list of things to buy. We needed the staples of life: milk, flour, eggs, bread, and so forth. I never want to over-spiritualize things, but the reality is, as children of God, we should ask Him to direct our steps, no matter what we are doing. I was determined to be led by the Spirit, so I prayed that day and asked Him to lead me and help me find all that we needed.

After I had asked the Lord to help me, I wasn't led to start looking for the first item on the list but rather for the flour. I made my way to the baking aisle and was shocked when I saw that the shelves were practically empty. There were no chocolate chips and there were no cake mixes. The yeast, baking powder, and other common ingredients were all gone. Far down the aisle, I spotted what looked to me like one lonely bag of flour on a shelf. I made my way there in haste and quickly grabbed that one bag and put it in my cart.

I was so excited about finding the last bag of flour. "It pays to listen to the Spirit's voice," I was telling myself. With so many people in the store, how had I been so blessed to get the very last bag of flour? I was rejoicing.

Just then, a lady was passing by at the end of the aisle. She looked down the row of empty shelves and then looked down at my cart. "Oh," she said, "that's the last one, huh?"

I said, "Yeah, I got the last bag of flour." As I was speaking those words, I heard the Spirit telling me to give my precious bag of flour to the woman. I had been so proud of myself and was looking forward to going home and telling Janet how the Spirit had led me to the last bag of flour, but now I knew what I had to do.

"You can have it," I told the lady. "Here, I want to give it to you."

"Oh no ! No, no, no, I couldn't," she said. "I just wanted to make a birthday cake for my grandchild tomorrow, but it's not the end of the world."

"No, no!" I insisted, "Take it! Really!"

She went through the formalities. "No, no, I couldn't. No, I couldn't. No! Well, okay, thank you. Thank you very much."

She received the flour, and I was happy to sow it into her life, but that meant I wasn't going to have flour to take home to Janet. I wondered what else I would find in short supply, but as I continued through the store, I was pleased to find everything else on the list. There were some eggs, there was some milk, and there was some bread.

Janet hadn't put any cereal on the list, but the girls and I love cereal, so when I came to the cereal aisle, I was delighted to find many different options still available. I picked up a few boxes and put them into my cart.

When I had everything I needed (except for the flour), I made my way to the checkout counter and began putting everything up on the conveyor belt. As I took out the boxes of cereal, I couldn't believe what I was seeing underneath them. Under those boxes was a bag of flour. It was absolutely astonishing! I knew for sure there had been only one bag in the baking aisle, and I had given that one bag to the woman. God is so awesome. He is the God of supernatural multiplication! I couldn't help but praise Him right there in the grocery store. His angels of abundance are working in our lives, even when we may not recognize it at first.

What I experienced that day was very much like a biblical miracle. It reminded me of the widow who had given the prophet the last of her oil and flour, and God saw to it that she never lacked from that day forward for herself or her son until the famine had ended. (See 1 Kings 17:7–16.) She was obedient to do her part, and God did the rest. Now it was our turn to need a miracle, and God was faithful.

My willingness to obey the Spirit in sowing a bag of flour resulted in a multiplied harvest of bags of flour. The miracle supply continued as people came and left flour on our doorstep. We ended up with so many bags of flour that we had to do some serious baking—and as we did, we had more than enough food to give away. When you live for God, you have plenty for yourself and plenty for others. This is true abundance!

Regardless of what I face in my life or what happens in the natural, I have angels watching over me. I have angels working with me, and I never lack for anything. Never.

Whether you see them or not, angels of abundance are released to work in your life as you obey the voice of God's Spirit. When you move in obedience, you move with the angels and the angels move with you!

Now prepare to unlock the last of the *7 Divine Mysteries* as you manifest unlimited abundance in every area of your life—and the lives of generations to follow.

DECREES OF ABUNDANCE

As you decree the following truths, you can expect to begin manifesting unlimited abundance. Spirit, let it flow!

- *My words in line with God's words attract angels of abundance.*

- *My actions in line with God's actions activate angels of abundance.*

- *I am blessed with an abundance of prosperity in every way.*

- *I attract abundance because I attract heaven's attention.*

- *I attract kingdom abundance. Everything I need is coming to me.*

- *I am focused on Jesus Christ and His abundant kingdom filled with life and goodness.*

- *I manifest the reality of heaven's unlimited abundance here on earth.*

CHAPTER 8

DIVINE MYSTERY #7: GENERATIONAL INVESTING BRINGS GENERATIONAL BLESSING

"Therefore know [without any doubt] and understand that the Lord your God, He is God, the faithful God, who is keeping His covenant and His [steadfast] lovingkindness to a thousand generations with those who love Him and keep His commandments."
—Deuteronomy 7:9 (AMP)

During the summer of 1998, my sister Katie, who was in her teens, was staying at Grandma Mills's house, and one day she decided to go out with some friends. Unfortunately, they were involved in a terrible three-car accident. Up to that point, the summer had been going great for our family.

Then this happened.

They had been driving down a two-lane highway, with a furniture truck ahead of them, when a couch suddenly dropped from that truck onto the road directly in front of them. The driver of the car in which my sister was riding suddenly had to choose between swerving right into a ditch or left into the oncoming lane. In that split second, she chose the other lane. What she didn't know was that a vehicle would be coming toward them in that lane at full speed. The two vehicles collided violently.

Both Katie and the driver of the car were severely injured. Also, Katie and other passengers were trapped in the back seat, and emergency crews had to use the Jaws of Life to get them out of the crumpled vehicle. Thank God no one died that day. It was a very close call.

Katie was transported to a hospital, where doctors examined her and gave their diagnoses. Her back was broken in several places, and they didn't give her much hope of ever walking again. Worse, perhaps, she was told that her female organs had been so damaged that she might never be able to have children naturally. It was a bad report that grieved the entire family.

My other sister, Sabrina, who was nine at the time, was also staying at Grandma Mills's house, and that night, she had a dream. In this dream, she was sitting on what looked like a captain's bed (a bed with a frame around it with drawers at the bottom to store things in). This bed was in a body of water, floating like a boat. As Sabrina sat there, she was visited by our great-grandmother, Natalie Wuerch. The interesting thing is that Sabrina had never met our great-grandmother. Neither had I or Katie or my brother Matthew. She had passed away shortly after my father was born, so even he didn't know much about her.

In the dream, Great-grandmother said to Sabrina, "I want to show you my treasures. You need to take them to Katie."

In the water around the captain's bed, Sabrina noticed beautiful, luminescent bubbles, and inside each of those bubbles was a different kind of blessing, including healings, giftings, anointings, and provisions. These were what Great-grandmother had referred to as her "treasures." Sabrina somehow knew that the bubbles represented our great-grandmother's prayers.

Grandma Mills was in the dream, too, and now she and Sabrina began to collect these treasures and put them into the drawers beneath the bed. When Sabrina woke up the next morning, she pondered the dream, but because she was only nine, she decided not to talk about it. She never mentioned it to Grandma.

ANSWERED PRAYERS FOR FUTURE GENERATIONS

Later, after Sabrina was back home, she mentioned in passing to our father what she had seen in her dream that night. Shortly after this, he called Grandma Mills and began telling her about Sabrina's dream and asking what she thought it could mean. Grandma was absolutely amazed by what Sabrina had dreamed because of something else that had happened that she had never told anyone about. Three weeks after her mother (my great-grandmother Natalie) had passed, a cousin told Grandma about a dream she had. In the dream, Great-grandmother Natalie was standing beside a bay. On the water floated many bubbles. An angel appeared and asked, "Would you like to know what these bubbles are?"

"Of course," the cousin replied, "I would."

"These are Natalie's prayers that are yet to be answered," the angel said.

Grandma remembered that, every night, her mother would kneel beside her bed and pray in the Spirit. Even as a young girl, Grandma had overheard her mother praying for her children, her grandchildren, and her great-grandchildren yet to be born. She would pray for blessings, giftings, anointings, and provisions to be given to them. She would pray in her heavenly prayer language, speaking the mysteries of God. These prayers were her "treasures." As Jesus said, *"For where your treasure is, there your heart will be also"* (Matthew 6:21 NIV).

Great-grandmother Natalie's treasures were a reflection of her heart. Those treasures were now available for each of us to access, and among them was the miracle Katie needed at that moment. The accident and its aftermath that had suddenly come into our lives had already been covered by Great-grandmother's prayers years in advance. There were now bubbles of blessing floating to us from the glory and being made available to meet the need. They were there just waiting for us to receive them—to pick them up and claim them for ourselves, just as Sabrina and Grandma Mills had gathered the bubbles and put them in the drawers of the captain's bed in the dream. This is a form of generational blessing, and it was there for my sister Katie.

When Sabrina shared her dream, the realm of the miraculous was opened to our family. Now, on a daily basis, we thank God for Katie's complete and total healing, but it didn't happen overnight. When I could, I would take my small piano keyboard into her hospital room and worship God at her bedside. Little by little, the miracle began to occur as God's anointing rested upon Katie and also guided the hands of the physicians. In the process, the scary words and gloomy predictions of the doctors were forgotten. Healing was our generational blessing, our portion.

Katie's spine was healed, and she began to walk again. To this day, she walks so normally that no one would ever know that she had been in an accident. She can dance, run, and leap. Hallelujah! Several years ago, Katie married and now has a beautiful family, including three precious children whom we absolutely adore.

As I reflect on Sabrina's dream, with its image of the captain's bed, I realize that so much about entering into the glory is about resting in God's unlimited grace and power and allowing Him to provide for us and meet all our needs. We need to rest completely in His presence, leaving all our concerns with Him, and simply receive the abundant provision He desires to give us.

CHOOSE LIFE

Generational blessings work. Moses said,

This day I call the heavens and the earth as witnesses against you that I have set before you life and death, blessings and curses. Now **choose life***, so that* **you and your children may live.***

(Deuteronomy 30:19 NIV)

We have many choices to make in life, and they will bring either generational blessing or generational cursing. The enemy will always try to get you to connect to the curse. He wants to establish and maintain a generational curse within your lineage. If he succeeds, you will sometimes have to deal with recurring negative situations, unusual patterns of behavior that cannot be explained in terms of what has happened over your personal lifetime. Sometimes the negative behaviors you fall into have nothing to do with you at all but are a predisposition you inherited from your ancestors who fell into the same things.

> *You show love to thousands but bring the punishment for the parents'*
> *sins into the laps of their children after them.*   (Jeremiah 32:18 NIV)

The enemy has tracked the sins, the transgressions, the iniquities of your family for generations, and he wants to keep you trapped in the same bondages that may have seemed easy stumbling blocks for your mother, father, or grandparents. And the enemy's motives are always the same—to steal, kill, and destroy. But remember what Jesus declares: *"I came that they may have and enjoy life, and have it in abundance [to the full, till it overflows]"* (John 10:10 AMP). God's will for your life is a full abundant life, a victorious life, a favored life, a blessed life.

In Deuteronomy 30, Moses encouraged the people to choose this kind of life and reminded them that their decision would not only affect them personally and presently, but would also impact the lives of their children and their other descendants. *"Choose life,"* he said, *"so that you and your children may live."* God is giving you an opportunity to do the same because now is the day of His favor. Now is the day of salvation!

> *I tell you, now is the time of God's favor, now is the day of salva-*
> *tion.*   (2 Corinthians 6:2 NIV)

When? Now.

> *"Now will I arise," says the LORD. "Now will I be exalted; now will*
> *I be lifted up.*   (Isaiah 33:10 NIV)

When will He arise? Now!

When will He be exalted? Now!

When will He be lifted up? Now!

You and I must choose to arise into the now with Him.

You may have really messed up in the past. You may have been stuck in a rut or buried under generational curses from years gone by, but now you have been given an opportunity. This is your moment. This is your day to choose life.

It's never too late to make this decision. Choosing life is choosing to live in generational blessing through the blood of Jesus and by the power of the Holy Spirit. It's time for you to take dominion over time, accessing the realms of eternity and seeing the blessings of God come in an accelerated way into your life and the lives of your loved ones. Yes, you can reverse the curse. Just come into agreement with the finished sacrifice of Christ on Calvary and with the life of the Spirit.

GOD'S WILL FOR YOUR LIFE IS A FULL ABUNDANT LIFE, A VICTORIOUS LIFE, A FAVORED LIFE, A BLESSED LIFE.

YOUR GENERATIONAL BLESSINGS

God truly wants to bless you. His blessings are mentioned hundreds of times in the Bible. This was not just a passing thought for Him.

Some people act like God's blessings are like a weather forecast: "There is a good chance of blessing today, maybe even a 65 percent chance." Every believer should know beyond a shadow of a doubt that the blessings of God are available to them. God is serious about blessing you. Christ paid the price that needed to be paid, and He wants us to receive His blessings 100 percent for every area of need. This is true for us, our children, our grandchildren, our brothers and sisters, and our parents. God is looking for a people who will choose to move in generational blessing.

Jesus gave His life so that you and your family members and your extended family members could live blessed and prosperous lives. If there was any dysfunction in your family's past or in the lives of your ancestors, reject those toxic habits and attitudes by breaking the curses. God wants to give you something new, and He wants to do it now. Say this with me:

"The new comes now!"

When the new comes, old things are passed away, and all things become new. (See 2 Corinthians 5:17.) And it can happen right now. Not in five minutes, five hours, five days, five weeks, five months, or five years. The new comes now...when we choose to move into it. Paul wrote:

> **Christ redeemed us from the curse** of the law by becoming a curse for us, for it is written: "Cursed is everyone who is hung on a pole." He redeemed us in order that the blessing given to Abraham might come to the Gentiles through Christ Jesus, so that **by faith we might receive the promise of the Spirit.**   (Galatians 3:13–14 NIV)

Something wonderful happened for you and me at Calvary. There, Jesus was made a curse so we could receive His blessings. Jesus was punished so that we could be forgiven. Jesus was wounded so that we could be healed. Jesus was made sin with our sinfulness so we could be made righteous with the righteousness of Christ. (See Isaiah 53:5; 2 Corinthians 5:21.)

Jesus died your death so that you could experience His life. Jesus endured poverty so that you could share in His prosperity. Jesus bore your shame so that you could know His glory. Jesus bore your rejection so that you could enjoy His acceptance.

The old self died so that the new self could live in you—and it can happen now. *"For we know that our old self was crucified with him so that the body ruled by sin might be done away with, that we should no longer be slaves to sin"* (Romans 6:6 NIV).

Things are changing now. Things are moving now. Things are shifting now. Sometimes we think, "Well, maybe my miracle is coming today, or maybe it will come later." "Maybe a change is coming today, or maybe it will come next week." God wants you to receive and welcome the revelation that things are happening in the glory right now. If you will enter into the now-realm of God, it will happen for you now.

NOW THE NEW COMES

Now the new comes. Now the new is here. Now is the time to choose life. Now is the time to live in the blessing realm. Now is the time to change the future for your immediate family and your descendants. *Now* the generational blessing is given to you.

Posture yourself. Get in position to receive it right now by faith. Open your heart and your hands to receive the generational blessing God has made available to you. He redeemed you so that the blessing given to Abraham could come to the Gentiles through Christ Jesus, so that by faith we could receive His promise of the Spirit. What was the blessing given to Abraham? It is spoken of in Genesis 24:1: *"The LORD had blessed him* [Abraham] *in all things."*

God wants to release a generational blessing to you that will bless you and your family in all things, in every way, in everything, and at all times. This is not an on-and-off blessing. It is for always and forever.

This means that the blessing God wants to release over your life is not merely seasonal. He is inviting you out of your season and into a new dimension. He's inviting you out of the earthly realm to live in the supernatural realm of His goodness. He is inviting you into the glory realm where the generational blessing of God can begin to flow like a mighty river that sweeps over your life. My friend Pastor Desiree Ayres says, "The enemy had a plot, but God has a plan!" The Lord God Almighty has already prepared a way for you, for He is the Waymaker, and He will see you through. Let those generational blessings flow without limit, flow without measure, overflowing with the abundance of God.

When generational poverty tries to show up in your home, tell it to move on because generational prosperity has taken over. When generational dysfunction tries to create chaos in your life, let it know that it no longer has any influence over you because the generational function and unction of the Holy Spirit are the new managers of your life and home. When generational sickness, disease, and infirmity try to invade your body, give them an immediate eviction notice because generational healing is moving in.

It's time to possess your territory. Bring in a heavenly atmosphere. Take hold of the blessings. It's not just for you and for today. It's for all generations to come. What starts now will overflow into succeeding generations.

> NOW IS THE TIME TO CHANGE THE
> FUTURE FOR YOUR IMMEDIATE FAMILY
> AND YOUR DESCENDANTS. *NOW* THE
> GENERATIONAL BLESSING IS GIVEN TO YOU.

SUNSHINE IN HER SHOES

Several years ago, I returned from a wonderful ministry trip to Budapest, Hungary, where we witnessed a genuine move of God. Many people came forward for salvation, and there were healings and deliverances, with many signs, wonders, and miracles. God was embracing people's hearts and revealing His power and glory. One of the most unusual miracles was when a woman's feet lit up, just as if she had sunshine in her shoes. Her feet glowed, and then her shoes began to radiate the light because of the brilliance of the glory coming through them. God certainly got this woman's attention, and during the service, she committed her life fully to serving Jesus Christ.

From Hungary, I went to Texas for a conference, and there, again, the glory of God showed up in a wonderful way. On Sunday morning, we seemed to touch the place of God's glory, the realm of eternity. There is no time in that realm, and no one is concerned about moving ahead or moving back. The only thought is to stay in that realm as long as possible. God's glory manifested, and golden glory began appearing on people's cowboy boots. "How appropriate," I thought, "in Texas."

As we were caught up in that glorious presence, I said to the pastor, "I needed this." It doesn't matter how much glory you've experienced or how many miracles you've encountered, every time you get into the glory, into the tangible realm of God's presence, you say, "This is exactly what I needed. God knew what I needed right now." I felt so refreshed, so encouraged, and so filled with life and strength. Little did I know that, in the natural, a difficult situation was right around the corner, but God knew. He always knows.

God knows the end from the beginning, and when He begins, it is with the end in mind. He has a plan to get you through the toughest situations and around the most difficult obstacles. His miracle access will be made available to you, and there will be signs and wonders and demonstrations of power when you need them. You will be given courage and boldness to take action, and you will be given strength to sustain you just when you need it most. He has it all prepared.

VISITED BY A PROSPERITY ANGEL[23]

Over a decade ago, I was ministering in Singapore at the Full Gospel Business Men's Fellowship Asia Convention. Leaders from many Asian nations were there, and Janet and I had the privilege of ministering to them. That meeting opened many doors for us all over the continent. After that, we went to Thailand, the Philippines, Japan, and many other nations carrying the glory.

Singapore is a financial center for all of Asia, and many of the Singaporeans who attended the conference were very wealthy. Many of the attendees from other countries were successful businesspeople too. On the very last day of those meetings, we were presented with a very sizeable and generous offering for our ministry. This was a great blessing.

We flew home to California, and while we were in the car driving home from the airport, we received a phone call from a ministry friend who lived in Florida. She said, "Joshua, I have a problem. I need prayer. My air conditioner has broken down, it's the middle of summer here in central Florida [where it is very hot and humid], and they tell me the unit is beyond repair and needs to be replaced. They are asking for $3,600 for a new unit."

I knew the woman didn't have the money in the natural and that's why she had called. But in that moment, I felt great faith that God would do a miracle for her. I said, "God's going to do it. He's going to give you a miracle."

23. I first related this story in chapter 4 of my book *Seeing Angels.*

She said, "I hope you didn't think I was calling to ask you for money. I wasn't. I just knew that you could help me pray. I didn't know what else to do. If you feel that God will do it, please agree with me in prayer." We prayed together in that moment and agreed that it would be done. When I hung up, I knew in my spirit that the miracle she needed was as good as done.

When we arrived home that day, Janet loaded the washing machine with one of several piles of laundry we had accumulated on our trip. We needed some fresh clothes right away because we were leaving that same night for Summer Campmeeting in Ashland, Virginia. We would fly into Washington, DC, then rent a car and drive to the camp. While Janet was doing the laundry, she agreed I should take the opportunity to go to the quiet of our bedroom and catch a quick nap. I was tired, and I soon fell deeply asleep and had the most wonderful dream.

The realm of God's glory opened for me, and I saw something I had never seen before. An angel of prosperity was coming toward me, and he was very beautiful. His hair was blond and flowing. Golden glory was in the atmosphere surrounding him, and there was also liquid gold pouring off his robes, and gold coins were spilling out from him in every direction. So much abundance...it was awesome! In that moment, I knew we had more than enough provision for all of our needs. No wonder God had said He would supply all our needs according to His riches in glory. I was seeing some of those riches.

These riches are not available to just anyone. Only through a right relationship with Jesus Christ can we enter into the blessings of such abundance. At that moment, when I saw the prosperity angel coming toward me, I was aware that I was about to receive a very special impartation. He was coming to give me some of the riches he carried. I was about to move all the way into this new angelic realm, and I was very excited about it. I was buzzing with anticipation.

Then, suddenly, I heard someone calling my name. It was Janet, and she was saying, "Joshua! Joshua! Joshua, wake up!" As I came out of the dream, I couldn't help but feel robbed of a glorious encounter.

"Janet, I was having the most amazing experience."

"Joshua, I'm having the most amazing experience," she said with such sincerity that I had to shake off the sleep and listen to what she was saying.

She told me that after the washing cycle was completed, she had moved the clothes into the dryer. Later, when she went back to take the clothes out of the dryer to fold them, she was amazed to find that each piece of clothing was covered with golden glory. This wasn't just a few sparkles remaining from the meetings in Singapore. There was so much golden glory that it was literally pouring off the clothes and pouring out of the pockets. Our laundry was covered with this supernatural sign of God's abundance.

I was so excited because I knew it was a confirmation of what I had seen in the dream.

"Janet, at first I was disappointed that you woke me up because the angel of prosperity was coming toward me, and I was just about to receive what he had. But now...I think we have it. I think we've got it!"

We were both excited, laughing and celebrating. It was a moment of realization that we had stepped over into something new. Instantly, we knew that we had to decree what was happening, and we agreed together that God was bringing us into a new realm of prosperity.

Then, as we spoke out this declaration together, something else happened. We suddenly knew that we had to do something about it. God had set us up. We now had to act on what He was showing us. As we did, we would not only enter into God's blessings for ourselves, but we would also secure blessings for others, including future generations of our family. We would set an example for our children and establish prosperity in our family line as a spiritual inheritance. Generational investing brings generational blessing!

FOUR KEYS TO OVERFLOWING ABUNDANCE

The following are four keys to overflowing abundance that we must understand and put into practice for generational blessing.

1. DECLARE THE ABUNDANCE YOU SEE IN THE SPIRIT

Determine to be open to God's voice and vision regarding abundance. Spiritual insight from God might come to you during the night as a dream. When you wake up in the morning, if you fail to declare what God has shown you, the enemy will do his best to steal it from you. Speak out what you have seen in the Spirit. Don't let the enemy tell you it was "just a dream."

People gifted in the prophetic see angels in the most unusual ways. For example, sometimes I see lights flicker around me. When I go into a room, I see white, sparkling lights that seem to be bouncing around all over the place. Other times, I see little flashes of light. Those flashes are tiny white flickers, and when I see them, I know that God has spoken to me. They are a sign of angelic activity, and I need to decree it. I need to speak it out. If you receive something from God in the nighttime hours or any other time, when that "knowing" comes to your heart, open your mouth and speak it into being.

"Why do I need to decree it?" some people might ask. Job 22:28 tells us, "You will also **decide** and **decree** a thing, and **it will be established for you; and the light [of God's favor]** will shine upon your ways" (AMP). Light represents God's favor, His abundance—and light is about to shine upon your ways.

There are many things that God wants to establish in your life, and He'll reveal them to you in the Spirit. You may see them in the Spirit, hear them in the Spirit, and/or know them in the Spirit. But again, that's just a first step.

God's abundance is for body, soul, and spirit, but you must access it to make it a reality in every area of your daily life. If something new in the glory realm is being revealed to you, declare it, and thus establish it. Decree what you know to be true in the Spirit, and God will make it work in your life. You must establish His abundance through your faith-filled decrees.

I had received the revelation that angels of prosperity were working in our lives. This meant that God was bringing us into more than enough, regardless of what it might look like at times in the natural. When God showed me that these angels of prosperity had been assigned to us, Janet and I began to declare, to ourselves and to others,

"There are angels of prosperity assigned to our lives." Until that time, I had never seen a prosperity angel, but the moment I saw him, we declared his presence, and because we declared it, we established it. From that day forward, prosperity has followed us.

The wonderful part about our realization of God's favor is that we both sensed it, and we both agreed to step into it. It's very powerful when a couple can agree on what God is doing in their lives. Oh, beloved, that's why God wants to give you a godly spouse. If you are married and don't have a godly spouse, God wants to change that for you. He wants to anoint your spouse with the power of His glory.

Pray for your spouse, and then, no matter how annoyed or disappointed you might become with your partner, keep praying for them. Don't curse; bless! Speak life into your spouse. Remember the principle of seedtime and harvest. If you are constantly sowing negativity into a relationship, what do you think you will harvest? But if you are sowing God seeds, you will reap a God harvest.

God knows what you're sowing. Keep sowing the right kinds of seeds, and you will eventually reap a great and wonderful harvest.

LIGHT REPRESENTS GOD'S FAVOR, HIS ABUNDANCE—AND LIGHT IS ABOUT TO SHINE UPON YOUR WAYS.

2. ACT ON WHAT YOU SEE IN THE SPIRIT

That first step of decreeing is an important one, but then you need to activate what you have seen in the Spirit. This means entering more fully into what God is opening for you. After Janet and I realized what God was showing us and began to declare it, we soon knew that we also had to do something about it. We must learn to work with the angels of abundance God sends into our lives.

Suddenly, the Lord reminded me of my ministry friend's need for an air conditioner. She had not called to ask me for money, but just so that we could pray together. We had prayed, and I had received an assurance that the need would be met. What I didn't know was that it would be met through me. That miracle was going to cost me $3,600.

How did I know I had to pay for the air conditioner? If it's never happened to you, it might be hard to understand. The Spirit dropped that impression into my spirit and Janet's spirit at the very same time. Janet was already so excited about the golden glory and had been asking me what I thought we needed to do with it. We knew this golden glory was miraculous; it was a heavenly substance and had within it a special anointing from God. It was actually tangible, so we gathered it all together, placed it in multiple envelopes along with little pieces of cloth, prayed over them, and then sent them out to people all around the world who had written for prayer and needed a miracle—just as the Scriptures teach in Acts 19:11–12:

> God gave Paul the power to perform unusual miracles. When hand-kerchiefs or aprons that had merely touched his skin were placed on sick people, they were healed of their diseases, and evil spirits were expelled.   (NLT)

We found out later that God did many miracles through those glory packages. But now God was asking us for $3,600 to buy an air conditioner for a minister friend. We had bills to pay and other needs to meet. Could this be His will? When it comes down to it, we have to decide if we really believe what the Spirit is speaking to us or not. It's easy to praise Him for the revelation of a prosperity angel being assigned to us, but now we were where the rubber meets the road. Did we believe or didn't we believe? God was asking us to give the money as proof of our faith.

Like most people would be in this type of situation, we had many questions, thinking, "God, You do realize that this is basically all we have in the bank account, right?" I thought we were coming into prosperity and was glad for the inflow. I didn't expect the outgo. But the Lord made His will so clear to both of us that we looked at each other and said in unison, "We're going to do it!"

We called our minister friend to tell her. It was about nine o'clock in the evening in California, and we didn't think about it being midnight on the East Coast. Our call woke her up, and I apologized for not having considered the time difference. Then I began, "We were having an angelic encounter—"

"Oh, please tell me," she said. "Tell me! Tell me! I'm not going back to sleep. Tell me!"

"I saw an angel of prosperity coming to us, and then Janet saw golden glory manifesting all over our clothing. Next, the Spirit spoke to us that we're supposed to pay the bill for your air conditioner."

Our friend began weeping and praising God over the phone. She said, "God has done the miracle!" We had a wonderful conversation. She was very excited, and we were too. What a joy it was for us to be part of her miracle. We were so thrilled. We told her we would put the check in the mail the next day so she could get it as soon as possible.

No sooner had we ended our conversation than we realized we needed to hurry to get to the airport on time. We went to change our clothes, and as I was putting on my shorts, I noticed there was a fresh twenty-dollar bill in the pocket. I knew it had not been there before. God was up to something good.

Someone might think, "You sowed a $3,600 seed and reaped a $20 harvest. Where was the angel of prosperity?" But we know God's Word, and James 1:21–24 says:

> *With a humble spirit **receive the word [of God]** which is implanted [actually rooted in your heart], which is able to save your souls. But **prove yourselves doers of the word** [actively and continually obeying God's precepts], and not merely listeners [who hear the word but fail to internalize its meaning], deluding yourselves [by unsound reasoning contrary to the truth]. For if anyone only listens to the word without obeying it, he is like a man who looks very carefully at his natural face in a mirror; for once he has looked at himself and gone away, he immediately forgets what he looked like.* (AMP)

When we begin to *do* the Word, the Word works, and we obtain the results of the Word. When we activate what we have declared, we enter into a place of receiving the harvest.

The Word also states, *"Who dares despise the day of small things...?"* (Zechariah 4:10 NIV). When God begins to move, He may do it in small steps. Even if your harvest looks small at first, receive it, enjoy it, appreciate it, tend to it, and give God thanks for it—which is the next key.

3. RECEIVE WITH THANKSGIVING WHAT YOU HAVE SEEN IN THE SPIRIT

Declare it, activate it, and then *embrace* it. Mark 11:24 says,

> *For this reason I am telling you, **whatever things you ask for** in prayer [in accordance with God's will], believe [with confident trust] that you have received them, and they **will be given to you**.* (AMP)

"They will be given to you." Yes! We must become generous receivers of the harvest God is bringing to us. When I found that $20 bill in my pocket and knew it had not been there before, I began to thank God, and I rejoiced over it just as if He had given me a million dollars. If we can see what's transpiring in the glory realm, we will know that every small step is leading to our full blessing.

I believe that when God introduces us to abundance, He teaches us step-by-step in order to see how we will react at every turn. Very often, we are placed in situations of testing. God is saying, "How will you react if I give you $20? Will you be grateful? Will you be thankful, or will you say, 'That's not nearly enough'?"

Our son, Lincoln, was very young when we received the revelation of the prosperity angels. That day, when he put on his shorts to go to the airport, the very same thing happened to him that happened to me. He reached into his pocket and found money there. I knew, without a doubt, that my seven-year-old son did not have money in his pockets. We all rejoiced together.

That evening, we boarded our red-eye flight and flew to Washington, DC. There, we rented a car and drove to our hotel just outside of Ashland. Even though we had flown all night, I set up my laptop because I had some office work I needed to take care of after having been on our extended trip to Asia. The first email that popped up came from the Full Gospel Business Men's group where we had just been ministering. It said something like, "The most unusual thing has happened since you left. This has never happened to us before. Even after you left, people wanted to continue to give to your ministry. There is additional money we need to send to you."

There is no way anyone could have manipulated the circumstances to make that happen. That was God. We gave Him all the glory, all the honor, and all the praise. We thanked Him for the amazing things He does. He is the God of prosperity. He is a generous God. He is the God of abundance. Likewise, when you experience any natural or supernatural prosperity, thank God for His faithfulness. After all, every good thing comes from Him. (See, for example, James 1:17.)

That was a very exciting email, and we were thrilled about the news of additional money coming our way, so we shared our testimony with others. But that was just the beginning. Remember, the harvest will come little-by-little, step-by-step, and God will see how you react and note your attitude toward the blessing that comes. That leads me to the fourth key to manifesting abundance—spread the revelation.

4. SPREAD THE REVELATION

GENEROUS IN SPIRIT

Proverbs 11:25 declares, *"A generous person will prosper; whoever refreshes others will be refreshed"* (NIV). We could paraphrase this verse as, "A generous person is a source of blessing and will be prosperous and enriched," or "People who water others will themselves be watered, reaping the generosity they have sowed."

You and I must become generous in spirit. As I travel around the world pouring myself out spiritually to the people of God and those I meet on the streets, I share God's blessings. I pour out what He brings to my mind, what He puts in my emotions, what He has birthed in my spirit. I bless others as I have been blessed, and I must do this.

However, as I have been emphasizing, that's not enough. Our generosity must manifest in the physical and financial realms as well as the spiritual realm. I make it a point to sow finances wherever I go. That does not put me in financial difficulty. On the contrary, as I sow into the glory, God keeps pouring more and more into me. Every investment I make in His kingdom comes back to me in the future.

The Bible speaks of scattering our seed abroad. (See, for example, Psalm 112:9; Ecclesiastes 11:6.) Why would we do that? Because we have no way of knowing which field will produce the most.

As you live your life in generosity, pouring out wherever you are impressed to do so, you are guaranteed a harvest. And you will find that generosity is contagious. The testimony you live speaks louder than the words you speak. Share your blessings, and you can't go wrong.

Again, when God does something for me, I testify about it, giving Him the glory for it. This breeds even more blessings. In a short time, we find ourselves in a cycle of prosperity, a cycle of continual blessing—overflowing abundance!

Janet and I had been believing for a very specific type of vehicle and hadn't been able to afford it until after we had sent the money for the air conditioner. Within a couple of months after our step of giving in faith, we had the money and the vehicle we wanted. And there was so much more that happened in the months that followed.

GENEROSITY IS CONTAGIOUS. THE TESTIMONY YOU LIVE SPEAKS LOUDER THAN THE WORDS YOU SPEAK. SHARE YOUR BLESSINGS, AND YOU CAN'T GO WRONG.

SO MUCH MORE THAN WE COULD ASK OR IMAGINE

The next spring, Janet and I made a ministry trip to Hong Kong, and the morning after we returned home, we were lying in bed talking. The first thing we do every morning is greet each other with, "God morning!" That really gets us off to a good start. Momma Billie Deck taught us to do that. Since God is good, we can wish each other a God day. Doing so can change your whole perspective.

We were still tired from the trip, so, after greeting each other, we pulled our laptops onto the bed and started going through our emails. There was a message from our landlord saying that we would need to move by September because he and his family would be coming back to the area and needed the house to live in. We had been renting apartments and houses for the entire eleven years of our marriage, and we were tired of moving from rental to rental, so we had started sowing seeds with a purpose. Whenever we placed our envelope into an offering, we wrote on it "Our Home." We were sowing, believing God to enable us to finally buy a house.

When you feel something in the Spirit, say it and pray it. It may sound absolutely crazy, but declare it anyway. Declare it as you are driving in your car or working around your home. God may inspire you to say some usual "stuff," ridiculous in the natural—but as you speak it over your life, you are setting the tone for where God is taking you. And I can tell you that He is taking you to a better place than you've ever been before. When you receive a revelation of God's holy angels working on your behalf and you take steps to receive the blessings they bring, that's all you need. Get hooked up to heaven; you don't need any other connection.

We had only a few months to find a new place to live. But Janet and I both knew in our spirits, and declared together, "We're going to move one more time, and this time, we're going to move into our own home." Then the landlord of our office building suddenly offered to purchase a house for us that she had already found, although we had never mentioned our need to her. The house was perfect for us, and she told us we could pay her back with monthly payments for as much as we were able to! Praise God!

A few months later, I went to minister at a small church with a membership of only about seventy-five people. At the very last session, a man approached me and handed me a check that was enough to pay off our new house. I had not asked for it, and I hadn't even told anyone the situation. I certainly hadn't asked anyone to pay off our home, but that's what happened.

Just like that, I had a new home and much more—we were debt free, and it all started with a $3,600 seed offering. As I look back over the grand scheme of things, the whole plan of abundance God had in mind for us, I consider that $3,600 seed and think, "You know what? I got a good deal," and I've been living in abundance ever since. I received over and above what I could have asked for. It is just as the Bible says. God blesses us with more than we can contain. His abundance is spilling out, overflowing on every side.

WHAT IS GOD LEADING YOU TO BELIEVE FOR?

God has abundance, and abundance is what He wants to bring you into. What is He leading you to believe for? Start putting your angels of abundance to work. Start releasing the strength of angels to manifest unlimited abundance in your life!

God's realm of miracles is for you, for your children, for your grandchildren, and for all succeeding generations. Let's pray about this together:

> Lord, I thank You for the miracle realm, the glory realm, the realm of abundance. Just as no weapon formed against us can prosper, no weapon formed against the members of our families can prosper. We declare and decree generational blessings over our lives. Let these generational blessings flow to our children, our grandchildren, and all coming generations. In Jesus's mighty name, amen!

Through generational blessings, your relatives can be saved. Hardened hearts can be softened. Those who are bound by addiction can be delivered; every ungodly substance abuse can be broken. Sick family members can be healed. Disease and infirmity will find no place in your family line. Instead there will be health and wholeness.

Beloved, for every negative situation and circumstance that you face, where there seems to an obstacle to victory, where there seems to be a demonic attack, an enemy assignment against your life, God will not only give you the victory, but He will also give you the authority to release that realm of blessing to others.

God loves you and is even now working miracles on your behalf. He loves your family members and is ready to bless them too. Nothing is too hard for Him. No mountain is too big for Him to move. If something is blocking you, speak to that mountain in faith and command it to move aside. God's glory is in you and causes you to triumph.

Get ready for a release of generational blessings!

First, prepare a significant seed as an offering to God, something meaningful and valuable to you. Do this as a declaration that the curse is broken. Don't say, "It will be broken." Instead, say, "It *is* broken. The curse of fear, the curse of doubt, the curse of poverty, the curse of sickness, the curse of dysfunction—all these curses are broken right now, in Jesus's name."

Then, make sure to continually come into agreement with the flow of generational blessings from heaven. If no one in your family has ever made this choice before, you can be the first. Establish it right now in your life and in the lives of your family members. God's Word is forever settled in heaven (see Psalm 119:89), but you need to settle it in your own heart and life. Let it be settled right now.

If your family members who lived before you were dedicated and faithful believers, you have their bubbles of blessing awaiting your discovery. These blessings are just like the bubbles (the treasures) that my great-grandmother laid hold of in prayer. Because of her faith and faithfulness, those treasures were available for us to access in our day.

BELIEVE GOD FOR A GENERATIONAL HARVEST

This is your day. Choose life. Choose to sow in faith. Choose to sow a miracle seed that unleashes a miracle harvest. Prepare to leave a legacy for those who follow.

Psalm 100:5 declares, *"For the LORD is good; His mercy is everlasting; and His truth endures to all generations."* As you sow, believe God for a generational harvest. Believe for a change in negative family situations. Believe that your obedience will bless those who come after you. Let's pray:

> God, I thank You that You have given us seed to sow. The promise of Your Word is that You will release more seed to those who faithfully sow what they already have. We release our seed for a generational blessing upon our families. Let this blessing continue into the future and into eternity, and cause a supernatural multiplication to happen, resulting in a harvest of generational blessing over and over and over again upon our family members. God, may this gift continue to give, so that a great harvest will be reaped.

> Father, as we come into agreement with Your Word, may there be such a generational blessing established over our lives

that we would know beyond a shadow of a doubt that this blessing is ours. It belongs to us. There is no fear of lack, no fear of insufficiency, no fear of not having enough. There is no doubt in our hearts about the miraculous, about Your supernatural ability. Right now, our faith is being enlarged and increased, and we say, "Yes" and "Amen"!

I urge you to give generously to God. Give rejoicing. And as you give, think of your children and grandchildren. Think about the obstacles that may have been there in the past and see the victory God is giving you even now. You are sowing into victory, sowing into miraculous release, sowing into breakthrough, sowing into the abundance of God.

Now, let this generational blessing affect those around you—your city, your state, your nation. May entire nations be touched and blessed and have encounters with the Spirit of God.

"Trouble chases sinners, while **blessings reward the righteous***"* (Proverbs 13:21 NLT). If *"the righteous"* describes you—if you are trusting in Jesus for your salvation, for your forgiveness, and for the supernatural power to live for Him—take hold of the blessings. Does this make sense? Absolutely! After all, Jesus said, *"Seek the Kingdom of God above all else, and live righteously, and* **he will give you everything you need** (Matthew 6:33 NLT).

"Everything you need"! There it is. Does this just mean spiritual needs? Not at all. I need a lot more than just the spiritual. If you don't believe my interpretation of this passage, do a little research. Look it up for yourself. Dig a little deeper. *"Everything"* means *everything*. The King James Version of Matthew 6:33 says, *"All these things shall be added unto you."* *"All"* still means *all*, even in the twenty-first century.

Both *all* and *everything* are inclusive. Nothing is left out. What things will God provide us with? Godly things, heavenly things, supernatural things, of course. *And* He will provide us with physical and financial blessings, favor, prosperity, all things, everything. Nothing is left out, nothing excluded.

When we seek God, focusing on His kingdom and His righteousness, when we pursue Jesus Christ, our perfect Lord and Savior who died for our sins and rose again to bring us new life, to bring us into resurrection glory, we can have it all—everything, nothing held back or denied.

The day Jesus was baptized, the heavens suddenly opened, and the Spirit of God descended like a dove upon Him. (See, for example, Matthew 3:16.) Just before Stephen was stoned, he looked up into the heavens, and they were opened to him. He saw Jesus standing at the right hand of God to receive his spirit. (See Acts 7:54–59.) When Peter was imprisoned, God sent an angel to bring him out of the prison and into freedom so he could continue his ministry of spreading the gospel. (See Acts 12:4–11.) In the same way, God is prepared to open the heavens over your life and send angels of abundance to meet your every need.

Because God is more than able and because He is the Waymaker, when the situations of our lives look hopeless, we will declare change. We will declare that this is the day of God's favor. This is the day of His salvation, and our faith is now. Let's pray together:

Lord, I thank You for releasing miracles that will be uncontainable. Do the extraordinary. I boldly ask that You would do something that's so unusual, we would never expect this kind of blessing, a blessing that's beyond anything we could ever have thought of, asked for, or dreamed of receiving. I thank You for the generational blessings that flow through our lives. Right now, we connect to them. Let them be established and settled in our families, in our homes, in our daily lives, and in our ministries. In Jesus's mighty name, AMEN!

Hallelujah!

Now all glory to God, who is able, through his mighty power at work within us, to accomplish infinitely more than we might ask or think.

(Ephesians 3:20 NLT)

You have now explored and absorbed all 7 *Divine Mysteries*! As you begin manifesting overflowing abundance in every area of your life, keep this book handy as a reference if questions arise or when others ask you about your overwhelming success. Whether it is in relation to your finances, health, relationships, job, ministry, or family, your life will exude abundance, and people will want what you have. And now, you know how to point them to God—the Spirit of overflowing, unlimited abundance!

DECREES OF ABUNDANCE

As you decree the following truths, expect unlimited abundance, now and for future generations. Spirit, let it flow!

- *God's divine plan for abundance will be revealed through my life and the lives of my children as a witness and testimony to others.*

- *As a child of God, prosperity belongs to me, and I choose to enjoy it.*

- *I believe in God's power to prosper me and my family, and because I do, prosperity flows to us from all directions.*

- *Financial abundance overflows for me today through my thoughts, words, and deeds.*

- *My relationships flourish as God's abundant favor rests on me.*

- *Abundance goes before me and leaves a golden trail behind me.*

- *I live in harmony with heaven's rhythms of grace and glory in abundance.*

CONCLUSION:
YOU CAN RECEIVE
WITHOUT LIMIT

"By [divine] revelation the mystery was made known to me."
—Ephesians 3:3 (AMP)

My prayer is that, as you've read through this book, each and every divine mystery that has been uncovered for you has become a divine revelation in your spirit. God is the Spirit of revelation, and I believe that He's been working deep within your heart as you've focused your attention to learn, grow, and ultimately increase in the abundance of His glory.

The revelation of abundance that God has been securing within you cannot be taken away from you. Even as your heart has opened up to be challenged by, and receptive to, His promises, new blessings are flowing your way. Old mindsets have shifted, former patterns and behaviors of insufficiency have been dislodged, and heavenly vision has been cast so you can enter into a new place of walking in God's overflowing goodness.

God revealed His mysterious plan of supernatural abundance to the apostle Paul:

This mystery is that through the gospel the Gentiles are heirs together with Israel, members together of one body, and sharers together in the promise in Christ Jesus. (Ephesians 3:6 NIV)

Through God's grace, you've been granted the privilege of receiving the gospel of Jesus Christ, which abounds with the manifestation of limitless promise. Quite simply, the greatest supernatural secret to unlimited abundance is to delight in the revelation of Jesus Christ Himself. He is the Word...He is the Way...He is Provision...He is Eternal Life...He is everything you need.

In another teaching about God's purposes, Paul wrote,

*God [in His eternal plan] chose to make known to them how great for the Gentiles are **the riches of the glory of this mystery**, which is Christ in and among you, the hope and guarantee of [realizing the] glory.* (Colossians 1:27 AMP)

When we choose to focus on Jesus first thing in the morning, and when we choose to focus on Jesus as the last thing we do at night, everything in between will be filled with the riches of the glory of this mystery—Christ's glorious presence in and with us, and the experience of abundant life in Him according to His perfect will. That is a promise. (See, for example, Matthew 6:33; John 10:10; Romans 5:17.)

Everywhere I go, people come running up to me, saying, "Brother Joshua, I need some serious direction for my life and family. Would you pray for me?" They want me to lay hands on them and impart something specific to help them, but when I ask how much time they've been spending in the presence of Jesus in the glory, the answer is often, "Not much." Instead, they have been very busy dealing with life's problems. I never ask that question to make someone feel bad, but it's a valid question and a serious one. We have to address issues that arise in our lives, but we can't neglect the all-important priorities of our relationship with God and of receiving His life-giving Word into our hearts and minds through divine fellowship with Him.

How much time are you spending in the Word? The more you get into the Word and the more the Word gets into you, when you face difficult situations in life, you will know what to do. At the very least, you will know that God is with you and that He will see you through.

We all face tough decisions. We all experience moments when we feel as if we are between the proverbial rock and hard place. The difference is, when your heart and mind are filled with the glory of God, that glory will bubble up from your innermost being in the most troublesome of times, and the rivers of living water will keep you full of hope and moving forward. The presence of Christ will illuminate you and show you what to do. However, God can't do this for you if you are not diligently pursuing Him. He can't do it unless you're willing to spend time with Him in prayer, to set aside moments to soak in His loving presence, and to read, study, and memorize His Word each morning and night.

I'm not saying that you have to read a certain number of chapters of the Bible per day. You have, no doubt, placed some expectations on yourself regarding how you "should" be reading the Bible, and those expectations may be keeping you from actually reading the Word if you don't think you can live up to your plan. The secret is to get into the Word whenever you can. Get into the Word and get it into your spirit. Press in and receive your portion. Wise people make reading the Word a priority.

Those who are focused on what is important to God are destined for bountiful blessings. Those who meditate on what is on God's mind at the moment will be abundantly provided for. In fact, God says, *"That person is like a tree planted by streams of water, which yields its fruit in season and whose leaf does not wither—whatever they do prospers"* (Psalm 1:3 NIV).

Put yourself in this promise. Say, "I will be like a tree planted by streams of water, which yields its fruit in each season; my leaves will never wither, and whatever I do will prosper. I accept God's promise. I will prosper. Why will I prosper? Because the Spirit and the Word are prospering in me. The seed of God's Word deposited into my life will cause a harvest of glory to be seen in me. And whatever I do will prosper." (See Isaiah 55:11.)

THE SECRET IS TO LIVE IN THE GLORY OF GOD'S ABUNDANCE EVERY DAY.

Your season is changing now. I can hear the Spirit prophetically speaking and calling you into a new dimension of His overflowing abundance. He is saying, "Come up here. Rise up higher. Lift your eyes toward the heavens and generously receive My overflowing goodness. There is no limit to how much you can receive. There is abundance for your spirit. There is abundance for your mind. There is abundance for your emotions. There is abundance for your physical needs. Enter into My glory and allow My abundance to enter into You with ease. Your days of lack are over as you choose to trust My Word. The enemy cannot stop the flow of My abundance in your life as you abide in Me. Follow My ways and learn to be led by Me. You will discover new places of plentiful provision as You receive My vision. Walk in unlimited abundance. Live in it...and allow it to overflow in every way, for these are your greatest days!"

Hallelujah!

Now that we have unlocked all 7 *Divine Mysteries* according to God's Word, allow the Holy Spirit to guide you into unlimited abundance each day! I rejoice with you as you experience overflowing abundance in every area of your life!

ABOUT THE AUTHOR

Joshua Mills is an internationally recognized, ordained minister of the gospel, as well as a recording artist and keynote conference speaker. He is also the author of more than twenty books and training manuals. His books with Whitaker House include *7 Divine Mysteries*, *Power Portals*, *Moving in Glory Realms*, and *Seeing Angels*, all with corresponding study guides and audiobooks, and *Encountering Your Angels*.

Joshua is well known for the supernatural atmosphere that he carries and for his unique insights into the glory realm and prophetic sound. Wherever Joshua ministers, the Word of God is confirmed by miraculous signs and wonders that testify of Jesus Christ. He is regarded as a spiritual forerunner in the body of Christ. For many years, he has helped people discover the life-shifting truths of salvation, healing, and deliverance for spirit, soul, and body.

Joshua and his wife, Janet, cofounded International Glory Ministries and have ministered in over seventy-five nations on six continents. Featured together in several film documentaries and print articles, they have ministered to millions around the world through radio, television, and their weekly webcast, *Glory Bible Study*. They live with their three children, Lincoln, Liberty, and Legacy, and their puppy, Buttercup.

www.joshuamills.com